Acclaim for Claude Hamilton

TOUGHEN UP!
BASIC TRAINING FOR
LEADERSHIP AND SUCCESS

"Claude Hamilton's first book is a huge success. I've read a lot of books on leadership but never one about what it takes to toughen up the heart, mind, and soul. These are timeless principles that our society sorely needs today. Claude teaches us that by reaching inside ourselves, we can become all God has created us to be. Thanks, Claude, for being a great partner in LIFE."
—George Guzzardo, LIFE Founder and
Policy Council Member

"If ever there was a person to write about being tough, it is Claude Hamilton. Countless times, I found myself cheering for Claude with tears in my eyes as I experienced his trials and victories. A life well lived requires mental toughness, and this book not only shares great stories of overcoming, but it helps you overcome too."
—Dan Hawkins, LIFE Founder and
Policy Council Member

"*Toughen Up!* is probably one of the most important and powerful books I have ever read on how to go from a dream through the struggle and all the way to victory. Claude Hamilton has outdone himself. This book just might be what everyone needs to 'toughen up' on their leadership and life journey. Having known Claude for over a decade, I have watched him apply these principles to achieve a high level of success, not only in business but also in his personal life. His message is clear, strong, and useful—capturing the essence of what 'toughen up' really means."
—Wayne MacNamara, Successful Entrepreneur and
Policy Council Member for LIFE

CLAUDE HAMILTON

TOUGHEN UP!

BASIC TRAINING FOR
LEADERSHIP AND SUCCESS

OBSTACLÉS
PRESS

First Edition, October 2013
10 9 8 7 6 5 4 3 2 1

Published by:
Obstaclés Press
4072 Market Place Dr., Flint, MI 48507

Printed in the United States of America

ISBN 978-0-9895763-3-8

Cover design and layout by Norm Williams, nwa-inc.com
Cover art and cartoons by Sonya Beeler, sonyambeeler.blogspot.com

To those who are out there in the trenches:
Now are your glory days, even though you may not realize it.
These are the times you will be most proud of.
I love you for it.

If you take the easy way out, life gets harder.
But if you take the hard way out, life gets easier.

Contents

Foreword

by Orrin Woodward

Claude Hamilton's life ought to be written up in every North American newspaper and magazine—not because of his amazing results in life, although they are very impressive, but more because of the nearly insurmountable struggles he had to overcome in order to achieve this success. Nothing has come easy for Claude and Lana Hamilton. Indeed, that is why I love the title of his new book because *toughen up* is exactly what the Hamiltons did to win in the game of life.

Since age twelve, when he joined the Canadian Royal Navy Sea Cadets, Claude has reached the top pinnacles of leadership in every field he has entered. The reason for his consistent success is described in detail in the book you hold in your hands.

The Eight Strengths will guide, challenge, and inspire anyone seeking the principles of long-term success. Moreover, the chapters are so engaging that I finished the book still wanting more. How Claude taught so many lessons in so few words is beyond me.

The teaching, however, is just the tip of the iceberg. Claude's personal stories anchor each of the Eight Strengths, helping the reader view the principles in action. If success is measured by how far a person climbs from where he started, then Claude Hamilton is one of the most successful people I have ever met.

With so many around him making poor choices and living lives of quiet desperation, Claude has set himself apart through the consistent application of his Eight Strengths.

On a personal note, I consider it an honor to have had a front-row seat in Claude's life for the last seven years. During this time, I have watched him apply each of these Eight Strengths in his life and business, choosing principle over short-term profit whenever they conflicted.

His friendship, encouragement, and attitude have been a huge blessing to me. Throughout many hours of life and leadership discussions with Claude, I had already heard many of his stories and all the core principles before. Nonetheless, reading them in this book—while visualizing the joys, pains, fears, and successes Claude must have felt—moved me.

Accordingly, I warn you in advance that *Toughen Up!* is a roller-coaster ride of powerful emotions as you empathize with Claude's dreams, struggles, and eventual victory. This is a book that you will turn back to again and again for information and inspiration on your success journey.

Thank you, Claude Hamilton, for having the physical, mental, and spiritual toughness to "finish what you started." Because Claude finished, others will be inspired to begin.

—Orrin Woodward, Chairman of the Board of LIFE Leadership and Two-time *New York Times* bestselling author

Introduction

FROM BASIC TRAINING TO BUSINESS

Leadership and success aren't unreachable goals that can only be achieved by a few people who know special secrets. It is possible for anyone to become a leader by consistently applying the principles of success. Too often the difference between those who live up to their full leadership potential and those who fall short is toughness.

To truly succeed in anything, a person will have to face and overcome real challenges. And only those who toughen up and triumph over the obstacles of life fully obtain their goals and dreams. I learned this in the military, and I've seen the same thing repeated in business and family. Success requires toughness.

My Story

By the age of twelve, I was involved in the Royal Canadian Sea Cadets, Canada's junior training program for future military men and women. While many other youths my age were playing at the park, socializing at malls, or hanging out with friends, I was polishing boots, ironing my uniform, and learning to march with precision.

Of course, not all teenagers in my generation wasted their time. Some were actively training in athletics and involved in sports teams or putting a lot of time into doing homework, learning to debate, or honing their skills as performers in drama or music classes and clubs.

Still others worked in part-time jobs after school. I participated a little in sports, clubs, and jobs myself, but my heart was focused on the cadets. During these years, I learned how important it is to keep trying even when things get hard. I discovered that success always requires a little toughness.

When I was thirteen years old, I went to a cadet camp in British Columbia for a summer. The military was supposed to fly a younger cadet and me from Thunder Bay, Ontario, to Victoria, British Columbia. Something happened, and we were told we would have to travel by bus instead. This required four or five days on the road with literally dozens and dozens of stops.

I had never traveled much up to that point in my life, let alone by myself on a bus. But I acted as if I had because I was the leader—of this twelve-year-old kid with me! That's pretty funny, I guess. But I was older, so I felt I needed to stay strong and set the right example.

That was a miserable, boring trip. But at the time, it seemed like an amazing adventure to us. We got on the bus and took the very back seats. We must have been a bit rambunctious because the man in front of us kept telling us to shut up and complained about us to the driver a few times.

One day when we stopped at a restaurant to eat, my friend and I noticed some video games in the lobby. We both got really excited. Remember the stand up video games that you could pump full of quarters? Well, we lost interest in food and became deeply engrossed in our games.

We also lost track of time, until suddenly, I looked up and realized the bus was gone! A wave of massive panic started in my toes and literally ran up my body and almost manifested itself in tears shooting out of my eyes like a water hose!

I was so scared. But I held back the tears in order to put on a brave face for my companion.

He did no such thing. He immediately burst into tears!

I knew I had to toughen up. I remember making a decision to pull myself together emotionally and perform. That was probably the first time in my life I had to do that as a conscious decision. Later, I would call this kind of behavior "keeping my helmet on."

I knew I had to do something fast, so I told him it was going to be okay (even though I had no clue if it was). Then I ran into the middle of the restaurant. I felt calm, though I probably looked like I was in a panic to the customers, and I yelled, "*Our bus left!*"

I am sure I looked like a school girl in distress, but I remember feeling in full control—except for a tiny feeling of panic in my belly that hadn't left since I realized the bus was gone. A man stood up and said, "I will catch the bus! Come with me."

With no thought of safety or who this guy was, my friend and I jumped in his truck and sped after the bus. We quickly caught up with it. The good Samaritan in the truck waved the bus down, and we got back on.

As we walked to the back where all our stuff was, I realized that the passenger in front of us must have known we didn't get back on and all our stuff was still on the bus. But he had said nothing!

As I said, later when I was in the military, I adopted the slogan "Keep your helmet on!" to describe the need to sometimes push down feelings of panic, buck up to whatever is needed, and toughen up.

When you're in an area where you could be under fire at any moment, it's not a good idea to take off your helmet. But some people do it anyway. When it's time to buck up, wimping out just won't do. But some people cave in to panic anyway.

That's not tough—and it isn't very smart. In business, when I see people relax too much instead of keeping their leadership edge, I sometimes tell them to keep their helmet on.

Somewhere along the way, I also found myself using another phrase, and using it a *lot*. The phrase is "Toughen up," and I think it captures a real truth that our whole society needs to adopt.

The physical side is to keep your helmet on so you're safe, but there is an emotional side as well. Too often people run into a problem and get emotionally flustered. They get scared of some challenge, or they get angry if they don't see immediate positive results. For example, in golf, you have to stay focused. If your first shot is bad, you need to be emotionally tough and make the next shot count. We need to keep our helmets on, toughen up, and stay emotionally focused.

Push-Ups and Pull-Ups

By the time I was seventeen, I found myself at basic training in Cornwallis, Nova Scotia, being rousted out of bed at 5:00 a.m. or earlier to run in formation, spending most of my days getting yelled at by drill instructors, and doing a lot of push-ups, sit-ups, pull-ups, and seemingly every other kind of "up" known to humankind.

The common thread of the entire experience at boot camp was the idea that all of us needed to "toughen up!" Our goal was to become a better version of ourselves than the person who walked onto the base on day one of basic training.

I was glad I knew how to hang my uniform the military way and fold my workout clothes just right, how to put a serious spit shine on a boot as quickly as possible, and how to get those corners of my bunk in perfectly folded shape.

The lessons from my years in the cadets made basic training a little easier. Those who didn't have such preparation frequently suggested that my background made it *a whole lot* easier. I found that even with my preparation from the cadets, it took a lot of hard work to toughen up, make it through boot camp, and really excel.

As the days passed, my aching muscles eventually found their groove, and I got used to the daily routine—something no amount of training can prepare you for until you just start living it every day.

Emotional Toughness Is Harder than Physical Toughness

Surprisingly, I found that the mental and emotional parts of basic training were far more difficult than the physical demands. I would later learn that the same is true in building a family or a business.

Boot camp was hard work, and I watched a number of people wash out, some of whom had prior training. Some who did well at the physical challenges still failed and went home because the emotional requirements were just too hard.

When I finished basic training and began serving full time in the military, I noticed that—just like in the Sea Cadets and at basic training—some people succeeded, while others didn't do very well. I asked myself what the difference was between those who were successful and those who failed, and I started making a mental list of key traits and characteristics of success.

I met my wife, Lana, at boot camp, and we eventually married and started a family. Once again, as I watched people succeed and fail in marriage and raising children, I noticed that many of the same traits that brought success in military service tended to build successful families.

When I was growing up, my family had more than its share of problems, so I didn't really have any close role models of how to do it right. As a result, I began looking for role models of leadership—in the military and the family setting. This added to my understanding of what works and what doesn't.

Recurring Lessons

I started my eight years in the navy as an electrician. But I didn't feel like I was really changing the world, so I set my sights on becoming a diver. After a lot of hard work and proving myself as a diver, I joined an elite unit in the Canadian armed forces, and the training intensified. Moreover, the actual operations we carried out pushed me and everyone on my team to the limits of human effort.

I don't want to say much about this service because it was always understood by those of us in special ops that what we did was not for our glory but for God and country, and our code of honor meant that we would keep it to ourselves.

I will say that this service reinforced my understanding of the great lessons of leadership and success because many of the same traits and characteristics I had witnessed bringing success in the cadets, at basic training, in military service, and in building a great marriage and raising a successful family were also the main things that brought success in the special forces.

Of course, some people apply these traits to one or two areas of life and not to others, so not everybody who succeeds in one thing will do so in everything. But with that said, the most important attitudes, choices, and actions of success in one area are pretty much the same in other arenas of life.

Those who are tough very often succeed, while people who don't ever toughen up usually fail to achieve their highest goals. When I set out to build a business, I found that the same lessons applied there as well. In fact, of all my endeavors, I'm convinced that building a successful business and going through the many ups and downs of raising a family take the most toughness.

A Definition of Toughness

But what exactly is toughness? In the military we thought of it as taking a beating and just keeping on toward the mission—pretty much no matter what. Over time, I've come to refine this definition a little: toughness is being able to take punishment and keep your original intentions.

I once read the book *Man of Steel and Velvet* by Aubrey Aude-lin, and I think it presents a pretty good summary of real toughness. A truly tough person is gentle and caring most of the time but knows how to stand up for something, over-come challenges as needed, and keep doing his or her best even when the odds are overwhelming.

> **Toughness is being able to take punishment and keep your original intentions.**

For example, when my son was born, I was so moved and happy that I cried, and I'm okay that people saw me do it. I sometimes cry onstage when I tell a story that touches me, and I don't mind if people think I'm emotional. It's okay not to seem tough all the time, especially if you really are tough when you need to be. Being soft is sometimes exactly what is needed to be tough.

Part of being tough is being true to yourself, including being tender when it's the right thing. Being tough isn't always about be-ing rough.

It is an amazing thing to stay focused on your purpose even when you have already taken a lot of punishment and can't imagine how to keep going. Yet some people do—the tough people.

Over the years, I noticed that those who succeed are just such people. In the cadets, at basic training, in elite forces, in marriage, in raising a family, and in building a business, a lack of toughness near-ly always leads to something less than success. If we want to succeed in life and as leaders, we have to toughen up.

> **Weakness of attitude leads to weakness of character.**

Weakness of attitude leads to weakness of character. It really does. Tough people have a tough attitude. On the shooting range, for example, when I was firing a weapon, the accuracy of my marks-manship went up and down slightly depending on my attitude. I know this sounds amazing, but it's true. A good or bad attitude will manifest itself in physical reality.

> **A bad or good attitude will manifest itself in physical reality.**

Most people think attitude and performance are separate, but they really aren't. They are connected, even when we don't realize it.

When a person has a bad attitude, it's easier to quit, it's easier to cheat, and it's easier to justify bad decisions. A bad attitude brings weakness. The good news is that a good attitude brings greatness.

The Eight Strengths

Specifically, I learned from these experiences that there are at least Eight Strengths of real toughness in leadership and success. When I tell myself or someone else to "toughen up," I'm really telling them to employ these Eight Strengths. Each of the eight is powerful in itself, and together, they make for a person who is truly tough—in all the right ways.

The Eight Strengths are:

- Attitude
- Courage
- Character
- Duty
- Honor
- Relationships
- Passion
- Tenacity

These might seem obvious to some people, but they aren't often taught in our schools or even our homes. In fact, nowadays many parents try to shield their kids from these lessons in order to help them have the easiest lives possible.

Maybe that's a good thing for some families, or maybe it isn't, but at some point, adults need to face the world as it really is, toughen up, and become their best selves.

Settling for Mediocrity versus Aiming for Excellence

So many people don't live up to their potential in this life. Too many of us settle for less than we could become. And when we live below our abilities, we don't do ourselves or anyone else any favors. The world needs us to live up to our best potential. The better we are, the more we can bless the world.

So when we settle for less than our best, we fail to serve as we could in the kingdom of God and the world in general. If we all did our best, the world would improve drastically—and quickly.

The problem is that giving our best is not easy. It's hard work, and it pushes us beyond our usual comfort zone. That's why only tough people succeed in giving their best to the world. We too often set as our highest aim a life of ease, a plan to do less than we can, or a minimum mediocre goal that won't require too much of us.

Sometimes people simply don't have a goal. If you don't have a goal, you will hit it with amazing accuracy. In our culture, we worry too much about not dreaming big. We tell people to "be realistic," but this is too often used to justify not doing our best. "Being realistic is the quickest path to mediocrity," as Will Smith put it.

Imagine how such thinking impacts our families, our marriages, and our careers. Do we really want the minimum out of life? Too often this is exactly what people aim for.

> **If you don't have a goal, you will hit it with amazing accuracy.**

But the tough people do it differently. They muster the Eight Strengths, dig deep, and reach for their best. When challenges come, they face them and keep going. Such toughness is desperately needed in our world.

Imagine how much better our political institutions would be if we just faced up to tough choices and made them sooner rather than later, or if everyone in business and family leadership bucked up and did the right thing even when it felt hard—*especially* when it felt hard.

I'm certainly not saying that I do this as well as I should, but I've noticed over the years that facing challenges head on is a lot better than trying to avoid them. I didn't write this book because I think I'm perfect at this—not at all. I'm writing this to myself just as much as to everyone else. We all need to toughen up, and we especially need to remember this during times of difficulty and challenge.

Everyone Is Capable of Toughness

The good news is that all of us can be tough. Toughness is not something we are born with; it's a decision. In the military, I was often surprised by who succeeded and who didn't. And I've seen this same thing repeated in business many, many times. For example, one person looks like he's weak, like he'll never make it, yet he just keeps going regardless of the challenges that come, and eventually, he's a great success.

Standing next to him in the line at basic training is a guy who looks like he can't fail. He's in good physical shape, looks strong, and exudes confidence. But three weeks later, to everyone's surprise, he washes out.

So if you don't think you're very tough right now, you're in the right place. Keep reading. By developing each of the Eight

Strengths covered in this book, you'll increase your ability to be tough when it really matters.

Toughness Is a Habit

Toughness matters. Those who choose it keep going until they succeed. Those who don't…well, they tend to face failure after failure in life. At some point, every success will demand toughness, and those who stand up and overcome their challenges are the ones who ultimately make it.

The Eight Strengths covered in this book are not only vital elements of success, but they are also essential facets of effective leadership. Real leaders learn and apply all eight. Moreover, truly great leaders become examples of all eight.

People who are genuinely tough in this way are inspiring. Tough people, like Georges St. Pierre, Terry Fox, and Wayne Gretzky, make us want to be like them in the most important ways. I know that some people might not think of Wayne Gretzky as tough, but I disagree. The brawlers who are usually considered tough can certainly take punishment, but they too often get distracted from their purpose.

Gretzky didn't spend much time brawling; he just ignored anything that wasn't about scoring goals. That's what toughness is all about. Gretzky was tough like Michael Jordan was tough because he always stayed focused on his real purpose. Real toughness means winning, not getting distracted by trying to prove yourself.

That's the kind of tough I want to be, and it's the kind of toughness our society needs right now.

Examples of Toughening Up

My greatest example of toughness is Jesus Christ, who leads any list of people who faced overwhelming punishment and just kept doing the right thing. Indeed, without toughness, Jesus never would have lived the life He did or set His perfect example for all of us.

Toughness is the leadership trait that makes all the others possible because without it, the rest of a person's talents don't accomplish much.

Another great example of toughness in my life is my wife, Lana. As I said, I met her when we were both serving in the navy, and she is one of the main reasons I began looking for opportunities beyond the military and ended up becoming an entrepreneur.

When we started our business, we were basically broke. We actually made what we thought was good money. Of course, as I mentioned before, I joined the military young, and where else will they pay you—with no work ethic, no education, and no experience—fifty to sixty grand a year?

I met my wife soon after starting basic training. I was there to focus on my career, and she was distracting me. Or maybe it was the other way around. Either way, we were there in the military, and no one had ever bothered to teach us the basics of life.

There was no class in high school on "how to be successful and have a great marriage." It seemed there was nobody around who had that information, or at least, *we* certainly didn't see anyone teaching it.

But Lana was tough in all the right ways. I mean, she is beautiful and wonderful and loving, but in addition to these things, she is really strong. She used to get up every morning, put on steel-toed boots and fireproof pants and shirt, and go to work in a really challenging environment.

At that time, they had just begun allowing women in the navy to be on ships, and she was lucky to be one of them—but the men weren't happy about it, and they didn't hide that fact.

Women were not really welcome there, and it wasn't a healthy environment. She spent more time with them every day than she did with me. She hated the way many of the men on her ship treated her, but she just kept going anyway.

When she'd cry about work, how much of a man do you think I felt like? I wanted to fix it, but I felt powerless. Though she kept at it, I knew we needed to look for something better. Her toughness inspired me. And her tenacity showed them what a strong person can do.

How Success Feels

Those of you who are going to really succeed in life will probably underestimate how tough it's going to be. But you may also underestimate how *awesome* it's going to be.

I wish I could let you know in words what it feels like to wake up every morning and hit your goals. It feels simply amazing. If you could feel it right now, you'd be incredibly excited.

It's okay that it's tough because it's also awesome. As Emerson taught, don't ask for an easier life, but rather ask to be stronger and tougher in your life. The feeling of succeeding never goes away. It feels just as good today as it did ten years ago.

When we started our business, I knew we had to succeed because I wanted to get my wife out of her miserable work environment. And if I'd known then how tough success was going to be, I'd have done it anyway. In fact, I think I'd have started sooner and worked at it harder because it has been so worth it.

Another example of toughness in my life is my friend, mentor, and business partner Orrin Woodward. I've watched him face challenges that would break most people, and he just woke up every day, put a smile on his face, and went through the day with his faith and

> As Emerson taught, don't ask for an easier life, but rather ask to be stronger and tougher in your life.

trust in God and doing the right thing. His example is inspiring to me. I'm so grateful to him for it.

I honor Orrin for blazing the trail and teaching me and so many others the right path to success. The thing is, he could never have achieved what he has done without toughness. But toughness doesn't just happen; it has to be a decision, and I've seen him make tough choices over and over.

I've learned from Orrin that following principle, even when it is costly or painful, is the high point of being tough. Doing the right thing, especially when it's hard, is vital to real leadership.

What I Want to Say about Toughness

If you take the easy way out, life gets harder. But if you take the hard way out, life gets easier. I was once invited to speak to a group of youth, and as I thought about the challenges (and statistics about the problems) facing today's young people, I just wanted to tell them one thing: "Toughen up! The world needs you to live up to your potential, and it's going to be hard—really hard. So toughen up, because you're up to it. You can do it. You can live an amazing life. You just have to get started, keep improving, never quit, and live up to your best."

I love the quote by Winston Churchill, another very tough leader: "Never give in, never give in, never; never; never; never—in nothing, great or small, large or petty—never give in except to convictions of honor and good sense."[1]

I wish I could get that message through to every youth and every adult in our world. The problems of the world aren't insurmountable. We can fix them. But to do so, we're going to have to do our best. We're going to have to push beyond our comfort zone.

We're going to have to develop the Eight Strengths and really live up to our potential. But here's the good news: doing these things is going to be a lot more fun than taking the easier, mediocre path!

The Tough Path Is More Fun

Here's the big secret almost nobody tells young people: the tough path is the most enjoyable path. That's what I've learned in basic training, in the Special Forces, and in building a business and a family. The weak path…well, it's not fun at all. The tough path is *awesome!*

As Robert Frost wrote:

Two roads diverged in a wood, and I,
I took the one less traveled by,
And that has made all the difference.[2]

Doing the easy things is usually a path to less happiness and success. Real success comes from taking the tough path, and it really does make "all the difference." If you want to live your best life, if you want to become the leader and success you were born to be, it's time to toughen up.

> **Here's the big secret almost nobody tells young people: the tough path is the most enjoyable path.**

This book will show you how. It introduces the Eight Strengths of Basic Training for Leadership and Success, and each lesson will significantly increase your ability to live your dreams. This book is meant to be a basic training on how to succeed.

Imagine it's a cold, Canadian morning. You wake up early, and the car window has to be scraped. You're miserable, but you do it anyway. You drive to the gym. You are freezing and hungry, but you do your morning workout. By the time you are done, you feel great. In fact, you feel fantastic the rest of the day.

Imagine, on the other hand, when the alarm rings, you turn it off, roll over, and go back to sleep. Instead of working out, you get a full breakfast, get a little more sleep, and don't have to scrape the windshield, but you let yourself down. So then you feel bad about yourself until you have a chance to correct it the next morning.

The hard way leads to feeling great because the road less traveled is the path of leaders. Not only does toughness bring more success, but it is a lot more enjoyable. It's more fun.

Dare to Dream Big

One of the saddest things about our world is that many people are encouraged not to dream too much or too big. "If you aim too high, you'll just be disappointed" seems to be the theme in far too many homes, schools, and organizations.

But this is the weak way. The tough way is to dream big and then go out and work, pray, and work some more until you fulfill your dreams. If you fall short, you'll at least have the great experience of really living.

To paraphrase Shakespeare, those who choose the easy path "die many times before their deaths; the valiant never taste of death but once."[3] Why would anyone choose to do anything except aim for his or her very best?

Each of us has great potential inside us. We just need to toughen up and start living like we believe it.

What Kind of Life Do You Want?

In my experience, those who aim high and work hard are happier than those who (often in the name of "being realistic") aim low and accomplish little. Yes, the high road is tougher, but those who toughen up and take it usually live truly great lives.

That's the kind of life I want to live. I don't always meet every goal I set or live up to every ideal I believe in—far from it. Sadly, I fall short way too often. When I do and I want to turn things around and get back on the path of real leadership, I look at myself in the mirror and tell myself to toughen up. I review the Eight Strengths, outline ways I can improve on them, and then get back to work.

I hope my thoughts on this process will be helpful to you in achieving your dreams and fulfilling your great potential. That's why I wrote this book.

The Contagious Power of Example

I know from long observation and personal experience that the Eight Strengths work. They are the basis of all toughness, the foundation of all success. If you apply them at higher levels than you are now, I believe you'll see your successes increase. If you don't, I'm pretty sure you'll see your progress decrease.

More important, however, is the impact your choices will have on those around you—in your career, business, and family. Those who apply the Eight Strengths are always on the path of leadership and success, and their example is contagious.

One of my deepest hopes, the reason I wanted to share the thoughts in this book, is that a lot more of us can be this kind of person.

So welcome to Basic Training for Leadership and Success! We're going to spend some great time together as we go through the lessons and exercises in this book. When we're done, you're going to understand what it means to be tough in the right way.

As you learn each lesson, you're going to have the opportunity to toughen up in eight powerful ways. I won't yell at you like a drill sergeant or make you do push-ups, but each chapter will help you on your path to increased toughness.

I won't make you wake up at 5:00 a.m. to read this or read it in formation while you run with everyone else who is reading it. And I won't check your boots to see how well they're polished. But if you apply the lessons and exercises here, you'll toughen up nonetheless.

And as I said, toughness matters. It will have a direct impact on your leadership, success, and personal happiness in life.

This is going to be a lot of fun because I never met a successful person who hasn't learned to be tough. So put on your running shoes, or better still the biggest pair of boots you own, and let's get started.

PART ONE

Rules of Engagement

Brave men are all vertebrates; they have their softness on the surface and their toughness in the middle.

—G. K. Chesterton

*Attitude is a little thing that makes
a big difference.*
—Winston Churchill

STRENGTH ONE

ATTITUDE

**"Change your life
by changing your attitude."**

When I first started building a business, I had a lot to learn. Fortunately, I had the right attitude—a sense that if I just kept going, I would eventually figure things out and succeed. So I listened to my mentors, and I kept going no matter what. It wasn't always easy; in fact for several years, it was downright excruciating.

But I kept the right attitude, and as a result, I learned a lot, even when I made mistakes or faced overwhelming challenges. For example, one night, I went out to have some business meetings. I had been diving for my military job, and I had some injuries: scratches on my face and such. Some of the water I was in was dirty, and the scratches had become infected and looked pretty bad.

I was out meeting people that night with a brand-new person that I was training to do the meetings. We had two meetings booked, one at 6:30 and one at 8:30, and I was excited to show the new guy how to do this. Actually, I was pretty new to it myself, but I was committed, and both of us were enthusiastic.

We got to the address of the first appointment, an apartment. I was positive about it all, which was good, but I didn't realize how much work was going to be required. I was used to jumping out of helicopters and doing all sorts of crazy things for a living in my navy job, and I assumed meeting with people and convincing them to do business with me would be easy.

I was in for a big surprise.

Facing Rejection

Our meeting in this apartment started to set me straight. In fact, to this day, when I drive past that apartment building, it still gives me shudders. We went up to the building, found the right apartment, and knocked on the door.

Our host answered, and we all introduced ourselves. He had us take our shoes off so we wouldn't muddy the floors, and we started talking. He looked at me, scratched face and all, and pretty soon, he asked if we could do the meeting somewhere else. I said, "Nah, we're all right here."

He looked at me and said, "Man, you know what? I don't think there's anything you have that I'm interested in." So we put our shoes back on and walked out.

I was devastated.

Walking down the hall, I said to the guy with me, "I'm sorry. That has never happened before, and it will probably never happen again." He nodded.

We went and sat in a coffee shop for almost two hours and talked while we waited for the next meeting. Eventually, we called our next appointment and asked if we could come a bit early.

We went over, and I felt pretty good about it. It was a nicer house, a split level. There was one staircase going down and one going up.

The man we were planning to meet with was standing at the top of his stairs to greet us, and he looked down as we were climbing the stairs. He just took one look at my face and said, "Hey, you know what? I'm really uncomfortable with you being in my house.

My wife and kids are here. Maybe we should just call it quits right now."

At that moment, I realized how I must have looked. I had my head shaved in the most severe military fashion, I was lean and tan from all the training, and I had terrible, infected scratches. So I looked like what I was: a trained warrior.

Or maybe I looked like a criminal or something. I don't know. When the guy refused to meet, I walked out of there, said good night to the trainee, and went home feeling overwhelmed. Rejection is hard, and everyone who has ever truly succeeded in life has had to face and overcome it. But knowing that doesn't make it easier.

Just Keep Trying

Fortunately, I had an appointment with a mentor who was coming out to see me two weeks later and had already bought the airplane ticket, so I couldn't quit. Otherwise, I think I might have been done.

Like I said, rejection is hard, and I slept poorly that night wondering if I should quit. But then the next day, my wife had to get up, put on her steel-toed boots and fireproof clothes, and go to work to be hassled by the guys there. I knew I just had to keep going and figure out how to get good at this new business so I could get her out of that situation.

I also knew, from my military experience, that this challenge I was facing wasn't going to magically disappear if I just chose a different career path.

I understood that there is a learning curve in any business or career and that if I gave up now, I'd

> To think that I might have missed it all just because rejection is hard— it's enough to really scare me whenever I consider it.

just have to face this same type of challenge in whatever new path I chose. Or I could just take it head on right now and figure it out.

I decided to toughen up and keep working.

Years later, it almost scares me how easy it would have been to quit. I love my life, the friends and community we're part of, and the lifestyle we've worked so hard to build. To think that I might have missed it all just because rejection is hard—it's enough to really scare me whenever I consider it.

Good Thinking

I had learned from my military service that thoughts matter, that our thoughts determine our attitude. This is a good thing because we really do have the ability to control what we think.

The great Roman emperor and philosopher Marcus Aurelius said, "Our life is what our thoughts make it." He also said, "If you are distressed by anything external, the pain is not due to the thing itself, but to your estimate of it; and this you have the power to revoke at any moment."[4]

> "Our life is what our thoughts make it."
> —Marcus Aurelius

In the same vein, it was James Allen who helped me take a closer look at the words of God when he said, "As a man thinketh, so is he."[5] If we give in to the temptation to engage in negative thinking, we can really bring ourselves down.

But if we focus on doing the right thing and keeping our thoughts centered on the right things, we can get and maintain the kind of attitude that helps us stay on track.

One of the most moving quotations I've ever read comes from Viktor Frankl's book *Man's Search for Meaning*. Frankl wrote, "We who lived in concentration camps can remember the men who walked through the huts comforting others, giving away their last piece of bread. They may have been few in number, but they offer sufficient proof that everything can be taken from a man but one thing: the last of the human freedoms—to choose one's attitude in any given set of circumstances, to choose one's own way." [6]

Imagine what it would be like to be in such a circumstance, torn from family and all you love, not knowing what has happened to those you care about, cold and hungry and abused in a concentration camp. I know a fraction of how that would feel, at least physically, from my military training. But if it were real? I can hardly imagine.

I would want to be one of those who, as Frankl said, went around helping others. I don't know if I would be that great a person, but I do know that those who were such incredible examples had their attitude in the right place.

We get to choose our thoughts, and our thoughts determine our attitude. Then our attitude determines our behavior and the direction of our lives. As another concentration camp survivor, Alexsandr Solzhenitsyn, said, "A man is happy so long as he chooses to be happy." [7]

Anne Frank and Corrie ten Boom taught the same thing. Attitude is up to us.

I've always loved the great poem "Thinking" by Walter D. Wintle:

If you think you are beaten, you are;
If you think you dare not, you don't.
If you'd like to win, but think you can't,
It's almost a cinch you won't.

If you think you'll lose, you've lost,
For out in the world we find
Success begins with a fellow's will;
It's all in the state of mind.

If you think you're outclassed, you are:
You've got to think high to rise.
You've got to be sure of yourself before
You can ever win a prize.

Life's battles don't always go
To the stronger or faster man,
But soon or late the man who wins,
Is the one who thinks he can.

Attitude is so important. Of course, when we first started building our business, I may have felt a little too confident. But that soon went away as I experienced how hard it was. Likewise, at basic training, I watched a lot of people who were confident on the first day later lose their edge.

It's not so much how your attitude is when you begin something, but how well you keep the right attitude even when you run into difficulties and hard times. That's toughness.

> **It's not so much how your attitude is when you begin something, but how well you keep the right attitude even when you run into difficulties and hard times.**

As Thomas Paine said, "I love the man that can smile in trouble, that can gather strength from distress, and grow brave by reflection. 'Tis the business of little minds to shrink; but he whose heart is firm, and whose conscience approves his conduct, will pursue his principles unto death."[8]

Championship coach Lou Holtz put it this way: "Ability is what you're capable of doing. Motivation determines what you do. Attitude determines how well you do it."

Four Stages of Success

Kenneth Blanchard, author of the *One Minute Manager* series, teaches that there are four stages in any new project or endeavor. First, when we start a new path, we enter the Orientation stage, where our energy is high but our direction is low because we usually have unrealistic hopes about how easy success will be.

The second stage, according to Blanchard, is Dissatisfaction, which is the natural result of trying hard but meeting little success. In this stage, energy is low and direction is low, and the majority of people give up most projects during this phase.

This is exactly where Lana and I were in building our business. Blanchard suggests that the way to effectively tread this stage is to talk to experienced mentors, find out what they recommend, and follow their advice.

Our mentors told Lana and me to just keep working at it, to hone our skills, and that is exactly what we did. We kept meeting with people, and while many of the meetings didn't bear much fruit, we slowly learned how to be more effective. For starters, I realized that looking like a gangster wouldn't win me a lot of open doors.

So we just kept trying, even when we felt discouraged. Blanchard teaches that during this stage, it is helpful to clarify our purpose, work with others to help us feel empowered, and learn to be more flexible, among other things.[9] We worked on all of these.

> **"I love [those] that can smile in trouble."**
> **—Thomas Paine**

The third stage of any new endeavor is what Blanchard calls Resolution. This occurs when our continued work leads to some success, we gain the needed skills, and we begin to envision a successful future ahead. At this point, energy is still lower than it should be, but direction is high because we become clear about what is needed.

Some people still give up during this stage, once they realize what it will take to accomplish their goals. But those who stick with it through the Resolution stage do so knowing what they want—and how to get it.

This leads to the fourth phase, Production, where energy and direction are both high and we start putting together one success after another. This soon turns to consistency, and while it still takes hard work, the Production stage is usually a lot of fun for most people. The goal is to remain in this stage as long as possible.

The Power of Attitude

The key to all of this is to have the right attitude throughout. In short, we need to learn to adopt the attitude of the Production stage (high energy and high direction and purpose) and keep it strong during the Orientation, Dissatisfaction, and Resolution stages.

Good mentors know that it is helpful to teach their mentees to get through the Dissatisfaction stage as quickly as possible. This is nearly always a matter of the right attitude.

During basic training, those who kept the right attitude were able to progress through these stages and stay positive. Others struggled, and some washed out.

Mahatma Gandhi, who certainly faced his share of challenges in life, gave the following counsel: "Keep your thoughts positive because your thoughts become your words. Keep your words positive because your words become your behavior. Keep your behavior positive because your behavior becomes your habits. Keep your habits positive because your habits become

> **Don't let circumstances determine your attitude.**

your values. Keep your values positive because your values become your destiny."

Stephen Covey summarized the whole concept of keeping a great attitude in the first of his Seven Habits of highly effective people. The first habit is simply, "Be proactive." In other words, don't let circumstances determine your attitude.

Instead, choose the right attitude and let everything else take care of itself. This is incredibly valuable wisdom.

Finding Our Purpose

For Lana and me, it took a while to get to this point. I watched something on television that said the person who stays home with his or her kids will spend more time with them by the age of three than someone who has a nine-to-five job will by the time the child leaves home at age eighteen. That just floored me. I was stunned.

I told my wife, "We've got to do something. If we both work and we rent out the mom-and-dad job during the day to the lowest bidder, then we'll have more money. We can go to Disneyland in the summer, maybe have two cars in the family, and the kids can play hockey instead of soccer. But we'll miss out on most of our kids' lives."

I was going through a big battle in my mind and realized that building our business was our best answer. That way, we could have time with our family and also the other things we wanted. I cared deeply about where we were going, and I cared about where I *could* take my family.

Remember, I had a pretty good career going in the military—a couple of my friends who are about my age are now generals and admirals—and at that point, I knew a long-term military career was possible for me. I was torn between that and my business. But I knew Lana needed a change.

The Right Attitude Means Doing the Hard Work

When Lana and I decided to really go for it in building our business, to push past Dissatisfaction and get the right attitude, it didn't automatically just happen for us. The first year, our business didn't explode. The second year, it didn't either. The third, fourth, and fifth years, we were just learning lessons. At times, it was miserable.

A lot of people would have quit. A lot did. But we didn't, and we learned many very important lessons during this time. For example, time is important. You do quantity, quantity, quantity, and then you get your quality.

> **You do quantity, quantity, quantity, and then you get your quality.**

But it's not only time, effort, and lessons. What's more important is that during such times of continued work, I answered the question: Who am I?

It just naturally came to me as I kept working. I learned that I would love to be with my wife and son and never leave the house again, but I have a bigger responsibility: I need to become a better man.

I need to set an example because someday I won't be around for my son; he's going to have to take care of himself. And how he does that and what he does in the world after I'm gone are what matters most about raising him. I *need* to set an example.

As I learned this about myself, something started growing inside me, slowly, consistently. I learned my life purpose, and I learned how to accomplish it.

Like I said, it didn't happen overnight for us, but the journey was incredible. I mentioned earlier that at times, it was miserable, but overall, it was wonderful. That may seem crazy, but it's still true.

I did something as we built our business and family that had never happened in the cadets, at basic training, or in the military. I found myself, I found my purpose, and I found my stride.

The thing is I don't think I ever would have discovered these things if it hadn't been hard.

Finding Yourself

Attitude makes all the difference. The tougher things are, the more opportunity we have to analyze our attitude and choose the right posture. Those early rejections defined me because they made me take stock of what I really wanted and decide whether to fight for what our family needed or give in and just let life happen to us.

Everyone makes this decision at some point, and most of us make it over and over as we go through life. Over time, it becomes easier and easier to keep making the same choice—either to settle for "whatever" or to aim for something higher. Each choice creates momentum, and as we choose to repeatedly aim higher, it eventually becomes natural.

The Wrong Attitude Causes So Much Pain

Another rejection I experienced during those early days of building my business remains burned into my mind. It helped teach me just how vital the right attitude is. I was meeting with a man to talk to him about what I was offering. As I got to his house, I saw a reject sticker on his car, which I knew meant the car was somehow not fit to drive.

I saw the television on and a big satellite dish, and I thought, "He's broke. He needs to make more money. Maybe I can help him." (Funny how a big investment in TV so often seems to go hand-in-hand with being broke.)

I explained my business plan to him, and we talked for quite a while. Finally he said to me, "I don't think there's anything I want bad enough to do more work for."

My jaw probably dropped in surprise. I didn't say, *Well, maybe to fix the brakes on your wife's car.* I was too amazed by his answer. Later, I realized that his attitude wasn't all that different from a lot of people's, but to hear it this directly was just shocking.

His wife was sitting beside him. She was quiet the whole time, and when he said that, her face just turned ashen. I've never seen a more helpless, hopeless look than this woman had when he said that. She was eight or nine months pregnant, and she was getting up and going to work every day. Talk about tough!

Her attitude was amazing, but at that moment, I could just feel her pain. Do you think she was going to work every day to win an office award, to prove to her friends she could do it, or to strike a match for femininity? No. Because of a lack of sixteen hundred or two thousand dollars a month—because she lacked the economic freedom—she had lost her personal freedom.

I couldn't believe it when he said that. It is one of the most amazing examples of the power of attitude I've ever witnessed first-hand. His attitude was simple: "I don't think there's anything I want bad enough to do more work for," even though his wife and family were struggling.

Because he lacked self-discipline and maybe some character and courage, and because he lacked some personal skills and the right kind of attitude, his whole family lacked economic freedom. And because they lacked economic freedom, they—above all, his wife—lacked personal freedom.

I left there feeling sad for that family. I didn't care if he joined my business or not. I just wanted him to do something, anything, to get a real life for himself and his family. But if he harbored that attitude, it didn't seem very likely.

Standing for Something!

You want to know something? Only those who are free understand freedom enough that they're willing to fight for someone else's freedom. It's all about attitude.

The biggest lie you'll be told in life is that the price of success is not worth paying (or maybe, "Mom, those are not my cigarettes; I'm just holding them for a friend").

> Only those who are free understand freedom enough that they're willing to fight for someone else's freedom. It's all about attitude.

The biggest lie is that the price of success is not worth paying, and the only people who tell it are losers. I don't mean they were born losers, somehow inferior. No way.

Everyone can be a winner. But those who believe that success isn't worth the price have chosen to be losers.

You'll never find someone who's won at something telling you, "You can't do it." But you talk to someone who flunked out of university and tell them you're thinking about going fifty grand into debt to go back to school, and they say, "Oh, that's not a good idea."

You talk to someone who has made it through, and they say, "You can do it." They may suggest other options that they think are better than going to university, but they believe in success—because they have succeeded. You'll probably never meet someone who has succeeded in building a business who will look at you and say, "You definitely can't do this."

"Most men live lives of quiet desperation," as Thoreau put it.[10] What are they desperate for? Money? Maybe. But do you know how many rich men are desperate? They live lives of quiet desperation because they are desperate for a cause. And the ones who are living for a cause will tell you how hard it is—and also that you are up to it.

Your Cause Impacts Your Attitude

When I put on a suit and went out to build my business every day, I wasn't doing it for the money. I was doing it to bring my wife home, so she could stop crying every day when she went off to work. What did I need to bring her home? Money. But I didn't look at it like that.

I saw it as giving my family what we really needed, mainly time together to live and grow and learn from each other. For me, this was a cause. And once I realized just how important it was, I loved doing it. It stopped being miserable.

> **It started to feel fun, even when it was hard. I just kept picturing the life awaiting us, and so I kept doing my best to make it a reality.**

It started to feel fun, even when it was hard. I just kept picturing the life awaiting us, and so I kept doing my best to make it a reality. And the more I thought about it this way, the more excited I got.

I would walk away from the rejections feeling nothing but excitement for the next meeting. I fell in love with helping people, and I knew that the more I helped them, the closer I moved toward our family dreams.

Somehow, at some point in all this, I realized that my attitude had taken a real turn toward positive. Actually, it was more like perpetual excitement. My daily meetings somehow changed in my mind from hard work to *saving humanity*.

Saving the World

I learned this phrase from one of my military leaders. For a time, I was the only Canadian on a team of Americans. We'd be flying somewhere in a helicopter, usually in the dark, and he would just start saying all kinds of things. He was a pretty good storyteller.

He frequently talked about all the significance in what we were going to do. He made it sound like whatever we were going to do at that moment in time—it didn't matter how small, like taking pictures or something—was important.

He gave me goose bumps and made me feel like we were making a real difference. He made me feel like I would do it if there were no paycheck. He made me feel like I was jumping out of the helicopter in the dark with a cape on.

> **He gave me goose bumps and made me feel like we were making a real difference.**

That's what he made me feel like, and I'll tell you why: because it was a cause. He was right. What we were doing mattered, but until he started talking to us about it, I didn't realize just how important our work was.

He helped me change my attitude and helped me realize that attitude determines how we approach pretty much anything. But one of the most important things he taught me was that our cause often determines our attitude. For example, in World War II, how many

> **Our cause often determines our attitude.**

who went over to Europe or Asia to fight did it so they could buy a new black Mercedes? None.

In fact, when they went to join the military after Pearl Harbor, many who had been rejected due to their health or age would just lie. They lied for the privilege of fighting. They lied in order to do push-ups and run sprints, carry logs through swamps and get shot at and sit for days in muddy trenches and eat rotten food and freeze in the snow. They lied because they saw a cause; they were called to a cause.

My Questions for Our Generation

When I speak to groups of Americans, I like to tell them, "Your country is doing a good job in lots of things, whether you realize it or not. As someone who has traveled a lot, I know this is true."

Then I ask, "But are *you* doing a good job? In your own personal life—for your wife, for your kids, for your group, for your best friends, maybe for some strangers you don't even know—are you doing a good job? If you want your country to be great, you have to start with you.

"Are you doing it for a cause, or are you doing it for money? Are you only building a business, or are you chasing your dream? Are you building a business, or are you fighting for a cause?"

People don't always like these questions, but our generation needs to answer them.

Let's get real, right now, right here. Is your attitude what it should be? Have you cried for your work yet?

Have the hairs on the back of your neck stood up yet because you feel like you're making such a big difference in your work, whatever it is? Does your cause inspire you to be bigger, better, and stronger? Have your dreams humbled you enough that you're willing to fight? What are you willing to die for? And what are you doing about it right now?

> **You will never, ever regret working your hardest for the thing you care about the most.**

I believe you die a loser if you find yourself on your deathbed without anything that you have been willing to fight and die for.

The good thing is that you probably don't have to die to live your purpose. But you probably do have to get fired up and get a dream and a passion. You probably do have to shed some tears and do some uncomfortable things.

But here's what I will promise you (the exact opposite of the biggest lie in life): You will never, ever regret working your hardest for the thing you care about the most.

The Secret Weapon to Getting the Right Attitude

That's what attitude is all about. If you have to constantly try to fix your attitude, you haven't figured out what you're really doing yet. You don't quite understand your deepest purpose—because when you know who you are, what you'd die for, and what you're going to do with your life that really, truly matters, your attitude will take care of itself.

In the meantime, it's okay to fake it till you make it, to do whatever you can to improve your attitude and keep doing your best. As you keep doing the right things and thinking about your dreams, eventually something will just click—and you'll find yourself.

When this happens, when you are doing what you do because it's a cause, a mission, a way to live your dreams and at the same time really improve the world, your attitude will take over and drive you to always give your best.

That's what the Production stage is all about, and the best way to get there is to keep doing the right things even when they're hard. If you hit the Dissatisfaction stage, if you feel overwhelmed or discouraged and just want to watch television and eat popcorn for the rest of your life, you've got to stand up, go to a mirror and look yourself in the eyes, and toughen up.

The rest of us need what only you can offer, and without your best effort, the rest of us will have a harder time of it.

Your Contribution Matters

We need you. Your spouse and kids need you, and your friends and colleagues need you. One of the best places to start is to realize that you have a deep purpose; there is a cause that needs your help. And when you find your cause and live for it, you'll find the most happiness and start to build your dream life.

If you want to have the most joy and fun your life can give you, find your cause and get to work.

If your life is perfect right now just as it is, then you might not need to change anything. But the people I've met who feel this way—that their life is great—are so busy building their purpose that you'd think they were just getting started. They aren't; they're just fully committed.

> If you want to have the most joy and fun your life can give you, find your cause and get to work.

If you want anything in your life to improve, you're going to need to change something in your life. And nothing changes things as quickly or effectively as adjusting your attitude.

As Katherine Mansfield said, "Could we change our attitude, we should not only see life differently, but life itself would come to be different. Life would undergo a change of appearance because we ourselves had undergone a change of attitude."[11]

Successful businessman W. Clement Stone counseled: "There is very little difference in people, but that little difference makes a big difference. The little difference is attitude."[12]

Everyone faces challenges in life, rejection, difficulty, and some hard times. In a way, life itself is like basic training. The tough people turn these things into bigger and better successes. And toughness often means continuing to do the right thing even when it seems futile or too hard.

In fact, doing the right thing is pretty much a cure-all for every problem. And the attitude that says, "I'm going to get up today and do the right thing, no matter what—and then I'm going to do the same thing tomorrow and every day after that," is almost a guarantee of greatness.

There's no stopping people who have this attitude, and it's almost impossible to stop whatever cause they've dedicated their lives to accomplish.

Attitude changes everything. As William Shakespeare put it, "All things are ready, if our mind be so."[13] Right on. "An attitude of positive expectation," Brian Tracy wrote, "is the mark of the superior personality."

We can all choose to be superior personalities simply by taking charge of our attitude. As Zig Ziglar noted, attitude determines altitude. I have witnessed this in the military, in families, and in business.

I wish I could convince you to do just one thing: Keep the right attitude. Choose to think the right thoughts. Keep doing the right things, no matter what. That's what tough people do, and this is why toughness is required for leadership and success. Over the years, in both the military and in business, I never met a good leader who wasn't tough in this way.

That's the first strength of tough people, and it works. If you ever find yourself struggling, for whatever reason, take control of your thoughts, put your attitude in the right place, and immediately get to work doing the right things.

No guts, no story.
—Chris Brady

COURAGE

**"When you hear them yell, 'Man overboard!'
what's your first thought? What's your first action?"**

A lot of people talk about courage, but in any Special Forces unit, it is just a given. It's expected. By the time you reach an elite level of training, everyone there is highly professional at what they do. In fact, if they wash out, they can usually go back to a pretty good situation and be at the top of their career.

Still, some of these people succeed, and others don't. And it comes down to attitude, as we discussed in the last chapter. But once a person succeeds in elite training, courage is just an expected part of the job. It's the same in business, I discovered. When you get to the very top levels of success, everyone has an amazing story of courage. Otherwise, they wouldn't be there.

Without courage, real progress and success just don't come around, at least not consistently. Luck does happen, but you can't count on it in every situation. Courage—now *that* you can usually count on.

Don't show me a person's résumé; show me what he or she is willing to fight or die for. Show me how much a person will keep doing the right thing even when it gets really hard. That's courage.

In elite military training, I learned that courage requires the right kind of balance. People who are too cocky eventually wash out. So do people who are too afraid and let their emotions take control. Courage requires us to keep control of our thoughts and to remain humble and teachable but still do the right thing.

Training for Courage

Many times our instructors had us run for hours. We ran, ran, and ran some more. Then, when we were winded and ready to just fall on the ground and gasp for air, they ran us even more. We were exhausted.

There was a lesson in this, something far beyond being in good physical shape. We were already in shape, but they wanted us to learn something, to know something about ourselves because when we were sitting there struggling for a precious breath and some-body yelled out, "Man overboard!" we had a choice to make.

We could sit and watch, try to catch our breath, and hope someone rescued the poor guy who fell overboard, or we could instantly jump to our feet, run toward the shout, and do whatever was needed to rescue the man in the water.

Our bodies cried out for us to just sit tight and get some air, but the whole point of the drill was to come face-to-face with our inner courage. Would our body win out? Would we sit and try to breathe? Or would we leap to our feet and sprint to the call for help?

Would courage or weakness rule us? It was a profound test, and we found out a lot about ourselves when we ran and jumped into the water, no matter how badly our bodies protested. Courage is like that: you don't really know if you'll use it until you do.

The Small Things

But you *can* train for it because when you do the right thing in the little things, you're more likely to do the right thing when the going gets tough. That's how the habit of courage is developed, when the little things don't take much courage, but you still just do the right thing.

Doing the right thing becomes habitual, and the little things create "muscles," muscle memory, and the pattern of doing it right, and this gets you in shape for the bigger things.

> **When you do the right thing in the little things, you're more likely to do the right thing when the going gets tough.**

This is a really big deal. Vince Lombardi said, "Fatigue makes cowards of us all." Toughness is about preparing ourselves in such a way that fatigue has less power over us. Some people probably think polishing boots or folding the blankets on a bunk has nothing to do with saving a life or running to rescue a man overboard when you think your lungs are literally going to explode.

But the truth is that these things have everything to do with each other. If a person cuts corners on the little things, if he trains himself to cut corners on things that don't really matter much, if he does the bare minimum just to get by in things that aren't too difficult, imagine how he's going to respond when something is really hard.

> **If we teach ourselves to make excuses and just do the easy thing in everyday decisions, we're probably not going to react with deep courage when something really difficult comes along.**

If we teach ourselves to make excuses and just do the easy thing in everyday decisions, we're probably not going to react with deep courage when something really difficult comes along. Courage is built day by day, by doing the right thing even when it doesn't seem all that important.

For example, once at a major business meeting, I noticed that some of the people didn't take notes. I know this is a dumb thing, but it really concerned me. It was like trusting my life to a guy whose boots were never polished. I'd always wonder if his tools were cleaned or if his weapon would jam at the worst moment because he hadn't taken care of something so small.

I looked at all those people not taking notes, and I thought about how unfortunate that was. If they didn't take notes, how would they remember what they learned? I really worried about it because I knew that building a business would be hard enough even if they did remember what they were taught. Without such wisdom, it would be even more challenging.

So why would they do that to themselves? Did they not really want to succeed? Or did they just not understand how important the little things are?

A few days later, I was at the dollar store, and I found some little notebooks. They were maybe thirty cents each. So I bought a hundred of them, for a total of about thirty dollars. Luckily my wife convinced me not to, but I was planning to go to the next meeting and hand them out to people who weren't taking notes. I was going to just shove them under their noses and say, "Here, take notes!"

Can you imagine how rude?

Another thing I see frequently is men handing notebooks to their wives and saying, "Here, honey, take the notes." And then the wife is writing away, and I'm thinking, "Well, hey, that's good. If you think like she does, then you'll understand your wife's notes. If you're a Mars guy, then that won't work." For example, I know when my wife and I take notes, she writes it all out, and I write in form. I don't get nearly as much from her notes as I do from my own, and she doesn't learn from mine anything like what she learns from her own.

Maybe Joce writes it all out, and Cynthia writes in form. Or vice versa. So if you think you can understand somebody else's notes, you go ahead and do that. You let her pick out your ties and shirts and everything. And she'll let you pick out all her clothes and makeup. I'm not saying that's bad; go for it. I just picture the shirt and tie laid out, and then the husband walks in the room saying, "I am a robot. I will wear whatever my wife says." And she does the same.

That's terrible. And then sometimes the wife wants to match. She'll be like, "Well, I'm going to be wearing this," and that's a hint. That's much better. You know what you want, she knows what she wants, and then you work together and do much better than either of you could do alone. But when one of you does all the little things, the other one isn't building the right habits.

Like I said, this probably seems like a little thing to most people. But that's the whole point! It's the people who build the right habits in the little things who generally have the natural courage to do the right things when it's really hard.

You have to understand how important the little things are. You've got to walk a mile to see a mile.

I'm not suggesting that we overdo everything. We have to have balance in life, and sometimes we just want to relax. I get that. But when we have a chance to learn from people who have been successful in something we want to do, we should treat it like a huge blessing and opportunity—because it is. We should hang on their every word and take notes so we can review them and milk every advantage and lesson out of their suggestions.

> **You have to understand how important the little things are.**

Again, courage is doing the right thing always, and when we do it in the things some people consider routine, we'll be a lot more likely to do it when things get tough.

Listen to the Right Mentors

Another seemingly small thing that is really very big is to truly listen to the right mentors. There is no substitute for experience, but the closest thing to experience is learning directly from those who have it. In the military, I paid close attention to the stories and ideas of those who had more experience than I did in tough situations. I learned to listen to everything they said. Sometimes a detail in a story they shared was hugely helpful in some later situation.

Learning from those who have been there, who have succeeded already on the path we're following, is an essential part of wisdom and leadership. For example, one of my mentors, Orrin Woodward, told me, "We want people to read, listen, and associate." He went on to say that these are the things that bring about real change. When we read and listen, we gain new ideas and a better understanding of how to do things. The same occurs when we associate with people who are trying to do the same things we are—even more so when we associate with those who have already succeeded.

There's a reason we need to read. There's a reason we need to listen. People read and listen in different ways, and that's great. We each learn our own way. For me, it's going to be a little different than it is for you. I always have a CD in my truck or car, and I listen to something whenever I drive somewhere. I'm listening constantly.

I also have an old CD player with a tape deck in it that sits on my desk. So instead of a six-figure big-speaker home music system, I've got this ghetto-blaster from the eighties. And I bought a Walkman. You remember those yellow Walkmans? I went online and bought one for like $160.

I used to have several of those lying all around so I could listen to my favorite old cassettes; I could make a killing off them now. Then I bought CD players, and I'm listening to something all the time.

Even when I'm working on other things, the audios are still in the background—and in the back of my mind—giving me lines and ideas, teaching me. I sit there and listen, and then all of a sudden, the same ideas will pop out of my mouth two or three days later.

I'll ask myself, "Wow, what happened? Where did I get that?" Well, I was listening to it somewhere, and suddenly, I'm up quoting it, wondering, "Wow, how'd that jump in there?"

Read Works from the Right Mentors

Just like listening, reading matters. I have a friend who is in business, and a few years ago, his business was just exploding. I mean, it was doing really well. I was very impressed with him, and as a mentor, I told him he needed to start reading. He responded, "Why? My business is exploding, and I barely read. Obviously, reading is not a key point."

What he forgot was that business is competitive, and there was someone running a competing business who *was* reading. So later, when things slowed and the other business was taking over his market, he realized what his lack of reading was costing him. The other business had better leadership, and the leader's reading depth made her a lot more effective.

I've heard him say that it cost him three or four years. He would be at the top of the market now, if he had started reading earlier.

I learned just how important this is by watching one of my mentors, Orrin Woodward. He's always reading. Almost every time I talked to him, he recommended something new to read. I finally got a notebook and made a list of every recommendation, and over time, I read everything on the list.

And don't be afraid to read the really good books more than once. I've read *RESOLVED* by Orrin Woodward many times, and every time, new things jump out at me that I didn't notice before. Just keep reading!

Leadership and success require wisdom, and that means reading as much as possible. And as I said earlier, this has everything to do with courage. Doing the little things because they're the right things to do...that's the whole point of courage.

I know I'm repeating myself, but sadly, not enough people seem to get it: If you do the right thing in small matters, you're going to be a lot more likely to do the right thing when it's hard. We build courage every time we do the right thing, even something seemingly as simple as listening to audios and reading important books.

> **Find a great leader with success in your field, and you're almost certain to find that he or she listens to audios and reads—a lot.**

In fact, these things are actually huge. Find a great leader with success in your field, and you're almost certain to find that he or she listens to audios and reads—a lot. This is just part of the program if you want to be your best self.

Associations Make All the Difference

In addition to listening to and reading works from the right mentors, successful people *associate* with the right mentors. You can learn a lot just by spending time with great people. If this doesn't make sense, try a little experiment. Go to your pastor or priest and tell him or her, "I'm going to read the Bible and listen to some Bible-based audios, and since I'm doing these things, I don't think I need to come to church on Sundays."

Or do Weight Watchers and say, "I don't need to attend the meetings; I'll just sit at home and read the materials." Guess what? It just isn't the same. It doesn't work. It's better than doing nothing, but it doesn't even come close to the success you'll have if you combine listening and reading with the right kind of association.

In short, association makes a huge difference. So read, listen, and associate. There is an old saying that if you look at the net worth of the top five people you associate with, you'll see a pretty good indication of your own net worth. This isn't always exact, but in principle, there is a lot of truth in it. What we associate with eventually becomes who we are.

My mum smoked for 420 years. Actually, it was only 42 years, but it was long enough that she eventually had to wear a mask to breathe at night. Then she made the decision to change, and she worked really hard at it.

However, some of her old friends didn't want to let her change. They constantly offered her cigarettes and tried to talk her into smoking again. Fortunately, she was stronger than that, but it just goes to show how our associations influence our lives.

But we get to choose our associations. For example, one day as we were building our business, a guy I was working with called me and said he wanted to talk. I asked if we could do it over the phone, and he said no. So we set up a time to meet, and I drove down to a mutual friend's home to speak with him.

He talked about everything but his reason for the meeting. (You can almost always tell when people want to discuss something ridiculous because they make a lot of small talk first.) We finally got down to business, and he said, "Claude, I want to take some time off from our business. For the summer, I just want to play baseball, relax, and have a break."

I asked some questions, and I could tell he was just using this as an excuse to quit. When he finished, I said something that most people would consider pretty mean if they didn't understand the power of association. I replied, "Ah man, we were doing so well. I was really relating to you, we were really getting along well, and I was enjoying my time with you. We've been kickin' butt. We were on a path to really growing our business, and I thought you'd become a leader in our company. I felt like we were going to be good friends. And now you want to quit. It's really sad."

He bristled and said, "Oh, so now that I'm not going to build the business, we're not going to be friends?"

"Well, I still think you're a cool guy," I said. "I'll wave at you at the grocery store and shake your hand. I mean, I really like you. But let's be serious. Friends spend time together. They do things together, and you and I aren't the watch-hockey-together kind of friends; we're the work-together kind of friends. I thought we might become more, but that would mean we keep doing things together."

He was mad at me, and he raised his voice as he said, "You only want me for the money. You're not a good friend. What's your problem?"

I responded, "You know what? I want you as a friend. And you don't have to do business with me to be my friend, but you do need to do something more with your life than play baseball and hang around at home watching television. I want friends who motivate me, friends who help me be better—and friends who I help become better."

Quitters Quit Everything

I continued, "My friends are people who have the same values, the same principles—they care about the same things. They are courageous. They want to do something important with their lives, not just make a living and then watch more television. I want friends who care about the things I care about or at least care about something deeply. I want them to be people I'm excited to have around my kids and my friends' kids."

I probably should have let it go at that, but I was a little frustrated at being called a bad friend, so I kept going. "And I don't want quitters around. The weak quit everything in life. Quitters quit everything! I don't want to be around people who quit. I don't want to introduce that into my life."

He was looking at me like maybe I was making some sense at this point, so I said, "You may think I'm hardcore, but let me explain to you what I do for a living. There's only one way to change a loser to a winner—only one. I know because I've worked hard to make this change myself. You can't give them money; you can't give them oppor-

The only power we have to change a loser to a winner is to change the way they think.

tunity. The only thing you can change, the only thing you can do, the only power we have to change a loser to a winner is to change the way they think. That's it. That's what our system does.

"It takes courage and work to keep trying, even when it's hard. I don't care if you want to take a break. I just hope you don't mean you're quitting. I mean, if you leave this because you want to do something you think is better for you, that's great. But if it's just an excuse for quitting, I don't really want to spend a bunch of time associating with you.

"I want to associate with people who help me do better because they have the courage to keep doing hard things. I want you to be my friend. I want you to be the kind of person I want to emulate and learn from, and I want to be that kind of friend for you. Think about it."

Maybe I was too hard on him. Now that I've had my share of success, I doubt I'd react that way. But at that point in my life, I was really trying to turn myself into a consistent winner, and I surrounded myself with friends and mentors who set an example of what I wanted to become. I knew how badly I needed that, and I knew it was important for him to learn, too.

Though I may have handled this too harshly, there is a principle here that should not be ignored. If you spend your time with people who are willing to give up when things get tough, their attitude will have a tendency to influence your choices. Part of courage is loving yourself enough to say, "I will not allow my goals to be hindered by those who aren't willing to achieve theirs."

There is a reason why so few people make it in Special Forces and only a few make it to the top of business success. Associations matter, and the more we can associate with those who are on the path of success—in whatever they've chosen as their field of focus—the better.

> **"I will not allow my goals to be hindered by those who aren't willing to achieve theirs."**

Maybe my former associate really needed to spend the summer playing baseball with his son, to strengthen that relationship or something. If so, good for him. But the principle remains: we can't keep on the right track if we let excuses rule.

We Can't Rest on Past Courage

Again, doing the right little things builds up a habit of courage. Churchill said, "Success is not final; failure is not fatal: it is the courage to continue that counts." All of us quit something at some point in our lives. But those who have the courage to forget their failures, refuse to rest on their successes, and look ahead and focus on doing the right thing now—these are the people on the path of success.

As I learned as a diver, "It's not the strength of the body that counts, but the strength of the spirit."[14] Mark Twain explained it even more clearly when he said, "It is curious that physical courage should be so common in the world and moral courage so rare."

Leadership requires moral courage. We have to stand up for what is right. Of course, it is important to do this wisely and effectively. It is important to think things through and be smart about how we use our courage. Churchill said it well when he wrote, "Courage is what it takes to stand up and speak; courage is also what it takes to sit down and listen."

The same thought was expressed in different words by artist and motivational writer Mary Anne Radmacher: "Courage doesn't always roar. Sometimes courage is the little voice at the end of the day that says I'll try again tomorrow."

A Deeper Look at Courage

Like most things in life, there is shallow courage and also real depth of courage. Things aren't always what they seem on the surface. For example, Twain said, "Courage is resistance to fear, mastery of fear—not absence of fear." That was certainly true on military missions, and it is frequently true in family and business leadership.

Nelson Mandela, who spent decades in prison for his political views, said, "I learned that courage was not the absence of fear, but the triumph over it. The brave man is not he who does not feel afraid, but he who conquers that fear."[15]

As author C. JoyBell C. argued, "Don't be afraid of your fears. They're not there to scare you. They're there to let you know that something is worth it." This is so true. Fear helps us wisely face reality, and it helps us see the value of what we are willing to fight for. We just can't let fear control us. In the same vein, James Neil Hollingworth said, "Courage...is the judgment that something else is more important than fear."

Harper Lee, the author of *To Kill a Mockingbird*, summed up this deeper understanding of courage when she wrote that courage "is when you know you're licked before you begin, but you begin anyway and see it through no matter what." In many cases, this leads to finding out that you aren't licked at all.

Courage and Independent Thinking

Another important facet of courage is that sometimes the biggest challenges are surprising. For example, the world-renowned designer Coco Chanel said, "The most courageous act is still to think for yourself. Aloud." This is really profound because leadership and success require us to think for ourselves, make our own choices, and take responsibility for our own actions.

> **As individuals, we increase or decrease our personal freedom to the extent that we take courage or shrink from it.**

Too many problems in our world exist simply because people are more interested in fitting in or impressing others than in standing for what really matters to them. Taking a stand requires courage, yet it is exactly what brings success.

Ironically, despite popular opinion, most of our schools teach us to think with the crowd, while in the top teams in the military, we were taught to really think for ourselves. Author Carrie Jones wrote, "The secret of happiness is freedom, and the secret of freedom is courage." We have our freedoms today because of the courage of a few great men and women—past and present. We will only keep our freedoms if we remain courageous.

As individuals, we increase or decrease our personal freedom to the extent that we take courage or shrink from it. Ralph Waldo Emerson shared this wisdom: "Whatever you do, you need courage. Whatever course you decide upon, there is always someone to tell you that you are wrong. There are always difficulties arising that tempt you to believe your critics are right. To map out a course of action and follow it to an end requires some of the same courage that a soldier needs. Peace has its victories, but it takes brave men and women to win them."

Courage and Love

With all this said, courage is ultimately connected to love. The mass of men worry themselves into nameless graves, while here and there, a great unselfish soul forgets himself into immortality.

The main purpose of courage is to help us stand for what we love, and when we truly love something, it naturally gives us the needed courage to do our part. The great Chinese thinker Lao Tzu said, "Being deeply loved by someone gives you strength, while loving someone deeply gives you courage."

In the military, some of the greatest motivations for courage are fighting for our families, our country, and our buddies. All of these are rooted in love, the kind of love that inspires ordinary men and women to do extraordinary things for others.

> The mass of men worry themselves into nameless graves, while here and there, a great unselfish soul forgets himself into immortality.

Sadly, this kind of love is too seldom found in our careers and corporations. Think of it! We spend most of our waking lives working with people and for companies without a lot of love. This is one of the main reasons Lana and I chose to build our own business. We wanted to do more than go to work, make a living, pay the bills, and try to eke out a few hours together with those we love the most.

We wanted to spend our time with our family and to build a business where our community of friends could love working with each other day in and day out. I experienced this in small, elite military units and at times in a special church congregation, and we wanted to build a business where this was the everyday culture.

This love drove my courage. I knew that if I kept trying, I'd eventually figure out how to succeed, and that if I succeeded, we'd achieve our dreams. I wanted this for my wife, for my kids, and for myself. I wanted to be surrounded by friends who wanted the same things. I loved this dream, and so I kept working at it.

Courage Means Taking Action

Nobel Prize winner André Gide rightly said, "Man cannot discover new oceans unless he has the courage to lose sight of the shore."[16] We must be willing to grow, take wise risks, and have the courage to truly pursue our life purpose, no matter what difficulties arise.

My business colleague Tim Marks is fond of saying that a successful life is like the voyage of a Viking. We don't always know what's ahead. But we know what is right, and so we take action.

That is courage.

We must take action. I've never met a successful leader who didn't exemplify the trait of taking action to get important things done. And, as we discussed already, those who take such action learn the habit of doing so even when things are most difficult.

> **It's easy to find people who want to have success. It's harder to find people who are hungry to learn, meaning that they are willing to listen and consistently do the things that bring success.**

It's easy to find people who want to have success. It's harder to find people who are hungry to learn, meaning that they are willing to listen and consistently do the things that bring success.

If things get hard, take courageous action. Be smart about it, but act. It is in action that great things are accomplished.

A Final Thought on Courage

Another essential aspect of courage is that it doesn't come from our abilities; it comes from the heart. I've already mentioned this in passing, but it's worth talking about directly. Napoleon said, "Courage isn't having the strength to go on; it is going on when you don't have the strength."

This is exactly what courage (and for that matter, toughness) is all about. Like I said before, when you're totally exhausted from running and running and running, and your body is howling at you to rest, and you hear the cry, "Man overboard!" what are you going to do? You feel like you don't have the ability to stand up, but your heart ignores your abilities and just springs up and sprints toward the yell. In other words, *heart determines ability.*

Whether you leap and run, slowly rise, or just sit there, the outcome will have been mostly determined weeks and months before by how well you did the little things that really matter. The habit of doing the right thing is the foundation of courage. So do the little things now—take courage and take action!

Fame is a vapor, popularity is an accident...
those who cheer today may curse tomorrow
and only one thing endures—character.
—U.S. President Harry S. Truman

STRENGTH THREE

CHARACTER

"I never met a broke person who didn't have cable."

I stared at the pile of bills and shook my head slowly. "There is no way to meet all these demands," I told myself. "If I pay all my bills, we won't have anything left for the things we really need."

I shook my head again, and I'm not ashamed to admit that I shed some tears.

I was broke. My business was growing, but unfortunately, my expenses were growing faster than my income. I was facing a number of challenges, including a major change in my business partners, a legal battle from some past business dealings, and the seemingly never-ending needs of a growing organization.

I turned off the audio CD I was listening to and made yet another list of bills, a futile attempt to balance my finances. After a long time, I pushed the piles to the side and leaned back in my chair. "What am I going to do?" I wondered aloud.

> "Whatever we don't have, we *do* have our character."

I had been trying to figure it out for days, and nothing was working. My chest felt tight, as it had for weeks. I took a deep breath and slowly let the air out of my lungs.

Then, finally, after days of frustration, I smiled. "When all else fails," I told myself, "our true character is revealed." I took out our checkbook and paid the first bill. Then the second, and I kept going until everything was paid.

"We'll just have to make do without groceries," I said. "These creditors don't even know I'm struggling. They'll never know what this cost me."

I put stamps on the envelopes and posted them, and then I returned to my chair. "Whatever we don't have, we *do* have our character."

An Amazing Thought

In one of Plato's dialogues,[17] Socrates has a long discussion about justice, goodness, and character with several men, including a man named Glaucon. At one point, Glaucon says something downright amazing. He claims that "no man would keep his hands off that which was not his own when he could safely take what he liked."

What a sad view of human nature! If this were true, we couldn't ever trust anyone with anything. I think Glaucon needed to make some new friends, if he could have, because his examples of how to be a good person were clearly lacking in character.

People do struggle to do the right thing, of course, and I've had my share of struggles as I've tried to build a character I can always be proud of. But Glaucon's idea that all men will take whatever they can get away with is, thankfully, downright wrong.

Frederic Bastiat wrote:

> Man can live and satisfy his wants only by
> ceaseless labor; by the ceaseless application of his

faculties to natural resources. This process is the origin of property. But it is also true that a man may live and satisfy his wants by seizing and consuming the products of the labor of others. This process is the origin of plunder.

Now since man is naturally inclined to avoid pain; and since labor is pain in itself; it follows that men will resort to plunder whenever plunder is easier than work. History shows this quite clearly. And under these conditions, neither religion nor morality can stop it.[18]

The problem with what both Glaucon and Bastiat said is that it isn't true of *everybody*. Men and women of character don't do this. I prefer what Orrin Woodward and Oliver DeMille said in their book *LeaderShift*: that while many people follow Bastiat's words much of the time, people who want real success and true leadership take responsibility for themselves. They rise above their temptations and want to earn what they get. They have character.

> **Character may be rare, but real leaders have it.**

Character may be rare, but real leaders have it.

Character Defined

There are at least seven different definitions of the word *character*, [19] and each adds something to our understanding of this essential strength. These include the following:

1. "The qualities that make a person different from others."

    This definition is important, especially in our culture, where we categorize and label everything from topics at school to personality types of people. The idea of character assures us that each individual person is unique, that there are as many characters as there are people.

I want to improve my character because there is only one of me, and the better I become, the more I can serve and bless the world in ways only I have to give. Nothing and no one can fully replace me, and if I don't live up to my full potential, no one will ever do the exact things I could have done.

In short, my character matters to the world because I am unique and irreplaceable. If I choose a mediocre or easy path, the things I leave undone can never be fully accomplished.

Understanding character teaches us to know people individually rather than label them only by personality type, career field, religion, political party, or some other description.

Still, as A. A. Milne suggested, "What I say is that, if a man really likes potatoes, he must be a pretty decent sort of fellow."[20] The great Russian novelist Dostoyevsky said: "If you wish to glimpse inside a human soul and get to know a man, don't bother analyzing his ways of being silent, of talking, of weeping, of seeing how much he is moved by noble ideas; you will get better results if you just watch him laugh. If he laughs well, he is a good man."[21]

Former US president Ronald Reagan quipped, "You can tell a lot about a fellow's character by his way of eating jelly beans."[22] Actually, he may have been serious about this. In short, each person does things a little bit differently, and this is part of his or her character.

Two Deeper Definitions

The dictionary continues:

2. "The particular nature of something…"

   Under this definition, our character is our nature. It is the way we naturally respond to whatever happens in life. If I want to improve my character, I need to use good plans, goals, habits, and momentum to improve my nature.

   When we say that a person has character or lacks character, we nearly always emphasize the good parts of that person's nature. In this way, the English language has a bias toward good over bad. But we can lose character by making the wrong choices.

3. "Strength and originality in a person's nature."

   I like this definition because it combines our natural strengths with our uniqueness. For me, this is the definition I usually mean when I talk about someone's character.

   The combination of strength and uniqueness is what makes us who we really are, and as we improve our strengths, the unique "us" can become truly great. I think this is what Martin Luther King Jr. had in mind when he said, "I have a dream that my four little children will one day live in a nation where they will not be judged by the color of their skin but by the content of their character."[23]

Additional Definitions

4. "A person's good reputation."

   I don't love this definition. I think a reputation is often a reflection of character, but sometimes one's character is worse, or better, than what people think it is. As the great basketball coach John Wooden put it, "Be more concerned with your character than your reputation, because your character is what you really are, while your reputation is merely what others think you are."[24]

Lincoln said something similar: "Character is like a tree, and reputation is its shadow. The shadow is what we think it is, and the tree is the real thing."[25] Socrates noted, "The way to gain a good reputation is to endeavor to be what you desire to appear."

But I think Thomas Paine said it best: "Reputation is what men and women think of us; character is what God and angels know of us."[26]

I would prefer to change this dictionary definition to "character: the strengths and traits that lead a person to deserve a good reputation."

5. "A person in a novel, play, or film."

When we get to know a character in a book or movie, we see his or her unique strengths, weaknesses, and traits. The same is true when we deal with people in real life. We also say a book is "strong or weak on character development," which is one measure of how valuable it is to us as readers.

It is interesting that people naturally want to see themselves and others improve and progress.

6. "An eccentric or amusing person."

We usually use this meaning of the word *character* when someone's strengths, weaknesses, or unique traits are very pronounced or extreme.

7. "A printed or written letter or symbol."

This meaning is interesting because people can also become symbols, some good and some bad. Our character largely determines what we come to symbolize to those who know us.

My Definition of Character

In addition to these official meanings of *character*, when I say someone is "a man of character" or "he has character," I mean he has integrity, loyalty, and strength. I mean he will stand for the right things, even when it is hard. I mean he is honest and dedicated. I mean I can trust him to do the right thing.

In the military, for example, I knew that if a man or woman had character, I could always count on that individual—in routine things and also in times of challenges and difficulty.

In short, I want to be a man of character, and I want to surround myself with men and women of character. I want my kids to grow up with such people in their everyday lives and as heroes and role models. The writer W. Somerset Maugham once said, "When you choose your friends, don't be short-changed by choosing personality over character."

Character and Adversity

I learned as a military diver that a person's real character is seen when he faces adversity. Helen Keller, who knew a lot about adversity, wrote: "Character cannot be revealed in ease and quiet. Only through experience of trial and suffering can the soul be strengthened, vision cleared, ambition inspired, and success achieved."[27]

I especially love how she said that in adversity, ambition can be inspired. Tough people have ambition, and they know how to stay inspired as well as how to inspire others. Heraclitus is credited with saying over two thousand years ago, "Character is destiny." Who we are creates who we will become.

> **Tough people have ambition, and they know how to stay inspired as well as how to inspire others.**

Paul Newman once noted, "A man with no enemies is a man with no character."[28] This is a particularly important reality because we should judge people not only by their friends but also by what they stand for and what (and whom) they stand against.

For example, a friend of mine told me the story of how he started a small philanthropy and spent a great deal of his time fundraising to keep it going and growing. He traveled to Edmonton, Alberta, to meet with a particularly wealthy potential donor who had expressed interest in supporting his organization and its cause.

After several hours of discussing the organization and its leadership, finances, and plans for expansion, the donor turned to my friend and said, "I'm very impressed with what you are doing. I just have one more question for you. In what ways have you and your organization been attacked and opposed?"

My friend was happy to report that they had received only support, no real opposition of any kind.

The donor looked at him thoughtfully and then replied, "That's too bad. Well, if your charity really amounts to something, you'll get your share of opposition. When that happens, come back, and I'll be happy to donate to help your cause."

With that, the donor ended the meeting, and my friend flew home. Needless to say, he was surprised by the turn of events. But more experienced leaders understand what the wealthy donor was saying because the character—of people and institutions—is truly revealed and defined only in times of serious adversity. And even more to the point, our character has not really been tested until it meets strong opposition.

Enjoy the Struggle

People only become great when they have to struggle, adapt, and overcome. So if you face difficulty in living your dreams and achieving your life purpose, congratulations! You're probably on the right track. At the very least, you're doing something right.

As the old saying goes, "If you haven't been misquoted, you probably haven't said anything that matters. And if you haven't been attacked, you probably aren't doing much that will really make a difference."

The good news is that adversity builds character. As the German philosopher Nietzsche said (and it serves as the unofficial motto of basic training camps everywhere), "What doesn't kill us makes us stronger."[29]

The writer Henry James said, "I don't want everyone to like me; I should think less of myself if some people did."[30] We don't have to go looking for enemies, but if we are doing important things, they will naturally come. And instead of worrying or cowering, we should be excited for the increased opportunity to do the right thing no matter what—and thereby improve our character.

> **We were born to do great things, and if they feel too difficult, we simply need to toughen up and get to work.**

Challenges, difficulties, problems, and hard things are a blessing in disguise. They really are. As Orrin Woodward frequently says, quoting the biblical book of Proverbs, "Iron sharpens iron." Challenges make us strong if we keep working toward our purpose. William Shedd said, "A ship is safe in harbor, but that's not what ships are for."[31] We were born to do great things, and if they feel too difficult, we simply need to toughen up and get to work.

Power and Character

There are at least two things that test our character even more than adversity. Abraham Lincoln said, "Nearly all men can stand adversity, but if you want to test a man's character, give him power."

Power tests our character because it allows us to do things without the negative results that often hold people back.

This takes us back to the beginning of the chapter, where we noted that Socrates's friend Glaucon argued that all men who are given the power to take from others without negative consequences will certainly do so. Again, I disagree. Many people will act this way, but those with character won't. In fact, people of character will be careful not to use their power in any negative or abusive way—and they'll be even more careful specifically *because* they are in power.

Plato said, "The measure of a man is what he does with power."

Mistakes Are Opportunities

A second great test of our character, even more difficult than adversity in many cases, is how we respond to our mistakes. It requires faith to forgive those whose mistakes have hurt us, but real leaders put the past behind them, forgive others, and move on.

Forgiving ourselves for our own mistakes can be even more challenging. Novelist Terry Goodkind wrote, "I'm afraid that we all make mistakes. One of the things that define our character is how we handle mistakes. If we lie about having made a mistake, then it can't be corrected and it festers. On the other hand, if we give up just because we made a mistake, even a big mistake, none of us would get far in life."[32]

Taking responsibility for our mistakes is one of the quickest paths to improved character. Journalist Joan Didion said, "Character—the willingness to accept responsibility for one's own life—is the source from which self-respect springs."[33]

This is a profound point and true. In our culture, we spend a lot of time trying to help children and youth—and adults, for that matter—have high self-esteem and improve their self-confidence. The toughen-up way, the boot-camp approach, is to earn your self-respect by your actions. When self-respect increases, self-esteem and self-confidence also naturally improve.

The difference is that instead of using techniques to boost esteem or confidence, tough people simply stop doing whatever is undermining their self-respect and simultaneously start doing things that really matter to their life purpose. In the process, their confidence skyrockets because they've earned it.

Harper Lee said, "Before I can live with other folks, I've got to live with myself. The one thing that doesn't abide by majority rule is a person's conscience."[34] When we do our best, we know we deserve to be confident.

> **Earn your self-respect by your actions. When self-respect increases, self-esteem and self-confidence also naturally improve.**

Just like adversity, mistakes are often a blessing in disguise because they cause us to stop what we're doing, take stock of our lives and where we want to go, and make needed course corrections that bring the results we really want. But the key to all this is to never give up on your life purpose, to keep trying no matter what.

Just Keep Trying

If you had told Lana and me in those first years of building our business how successful we'd eventually be, we wouldn't have known how to believe it. We just kept working at it, year after year. Maybe I was too dumb or hardheaded to do anything else. But I kept trying. I made mistakes, and I learned from them. I faced opposition, detractors, and attacks, and they all made me stronger. It was hard, and then it got harder.

I kept meeting, working, listening to audios, and reading. I kept going to meetings, taking notes, and then applying them. I looked for every opportunity to spend just eighteen minutes, or even less, with my mentors because I knew that greatness rubs off. And in all of it, Lana and I kept working.

The same was true in basic training. You could stop running, stop doing push-ups, stop trudging through mud, stop standing in the rain getting yelled at. You could stop a hundred things. But if you didn't, if you kept going, kept giving your best no matter what, you succeeded.

Everyone *can* succeed. But not everyone actually does. Those who succeed have a clear goal and a plan to reach it, and they just keep working until it happens. They treat setbacks like opportunities, or maybe they cry and whine, but they keep going anyway.

That's how success happens, after you just refuse to give up no matter what. As James Allen said, "Adversity doesn't build character; it reveals it." Actually, he should have said that it does both. But I understand what he was getting at because when adversity hits, you come face to face with who you really are, and you can either give up or get better. The choice is up to you.

Integrity

Another essential part of character is integrity, which comes from the root-word *integral* or whole. Spencer Johnson, coauthor of *The One Minute Manager*, wrote, "Integrity is telling myself the truth. And honesty is telling the truth to other people." Both integrity and honesty are part of having character.

"Somebody once said that in looking for people to hire," Warren Buffet suggested, "you look for three qualities: integrity, intelligence, and energy. And if you don't have the first, the other two will kill you. You think about it; it's true. If you hire somebody without [integrity], you really want them to be dumb and lazy."

Without integrity, character is impossible.

Authenticity

People with character are also genuine and authentic. Remember how many of the dictionary definitions of character touched on uniqueness? Men and women of character are themselves, even in a world where it seems like everyone just wants to fit in. C. S. Lewis wrote a great little article entitled "The Inner Ring," in which he taught that too many of us miss out on our potential because we're too busy trying to impress someone.

Lao Tzu said something very important: "When you are content to be simply yourself and don't compare or compete, everyone will respect you." That doesn't mean you shouldn't be competitive, but rather that you don't have to try to compete for popularity. Just be yourself, improve yourself, and like yourself.

Put your effort into your goals, your life purpose, and serving people, and don't waste time trying to win the admiration of others. Marcus Aurelius said it succinctly: "Waste no more time arguing about

> **Just be yourself, improve yourself, and like yourself.**

what a good man should be. Be one."[35] That's my kind of philosophy. Short. To the point. True.

Take action.

For example, the great writer Frederick Douglass said, "I prefer to be true to myself, even at the hazard of incurring the ridicule of others, rather than to be false, and to incur my own abhorrence."[36] When we are genuine and authentic, we are at our best.

Stand for Something

Perhaps the most important element of character is truly standing for something. Men and women of character believe in something important, and they take a stand for it and help it succeed. Nearly every great leader is ultimately defined by what he or she leads people toward, just as all real success boils down to the good it accomplishes in the world.

Great people stand for something great.

Together, these various facets of character help make us the men and women we should be, the leaders we were born to be, the fulfillment of our highest potential. Character includes the following traits:

- Doing the right thing, even when nobody will know
- Doing the right thing, even when there are no negative consequences to doing the wrong thing
- Being unique, genuine, and authentic
- Consistently working to improve yourself
- Strength
- Loyalty
- Standing for something that really matters
- Staying resolute in the face of adversity
- Turning challenges into opportunities
- Turning mistakes into opportunities
- Integrity
- Honesty
- Dedication to a cause that matters

Character is an essential strength for leadership and success. Jim Rohn said, "Character isn't something you were born with and can't change, like your fingerprints. It's something you weren't born with and must take responsibility for forming."

Sometimes we find hidden strengths in our character, if we just refuse to give up. For example, in the military, I took a preliminary course for advanced training that was really more of a test to determine who would actually continue on the diving career path.

There were twenty of us on day one, and we all came from different backgrounds. Some were divers like myself, some were search-and-rescue technicians, and others were infantrymen or medics. It was a good mix of people who were already quite successful in their current careers.

The goal of the course was to eliminate enough of the participants to get down to the final six. Only these would end up advancing.

If we made it to the final six, we didn't just get a raise or a new badge or another accolade to add to our file, but we got to actually change jobs, leave our current unit, and join a new unit with a different mission. Success in this training was therefore a huge personal accomplishment and also a game-changer in terms of our careers.

The course didn't run for a specific amount of time like most trainings in the military do. Instead, this one ran until the twenty course attendees got whittled down to six!

The rumor was that the record was twenty-one days…twenty-one days of constant pressure to quit. We all hoped it would not take that long!

Of course, if you quit, you weren't kicked out of the military or your current job. Nothing bad happened. You would just go back to being a "stud" at the top of your game wherever you currently worked. So the decision to continue had to come from deep inside.

All twenty people in the course were there because they were high performers at what they already did.

Day after day, we swam and ran and did every exercise imaginable in all sorts of conditions—day, night, rain, or shine. We went from classroom work to the range to the gym to running to swimming, all with very little food or sleep.

The instructors weren't trying to hurt anyone; they just wanted to keep the six most emotionally tough guys. And all twenty of us knew by this time in our careers that it wasn't going to be a physical decision as much as an emotional one. Although it was physically grueling, we had all been through many courses from basic training to leadership courses, and we all knew the key element was more emotional and mental than physical.

Sure enough, one by one and sometimes in pairs, people quit. When they were ready to give up, they just blew their whistle, and the instructors would very quickly take them away.

The twenty people became nine very quickly, and then it stayed like that for days and days. It just seemed like out of the nine, no one was ever going to give up.

As the work got harder and harder, and all nine people looked like they weren't going to blow their whistle no matter what, I began to think it would be me. The challenge was so difficult, and I started to weaken.

I knew as soon as I start thinking like that my self-doubt would grow and grow, so I squelched it as fast as I could.

But when you're cold and wet and tired and hungry and sore and you already have a good job waiting for you, it's easy to think about quitting.

Then I started playing mind games with myself. I said, "When the next guy quits, I'll go with him! That way, I won't be ashamed because I'm the first of the nine to break."

This plan worked pretty well because nobody else quit! We all just kept pushing ourselves, no matter what the instructors required of us.

Then one morning, still in darkness, we were awakened after just ninety minutes of sleep and told to get ready to run but to bring our wet suit, fins, and mask. This meant sometime in the next few hours, we were going to swim.

We started out running and then running more and more, past all the places where we usually turned around. I said to myself, "I'll run to the next landmark, and then I'll quit." But when I got there,

I reset my mind with a new landmark. I kept doing this for a long time.

We ran for the longest I had ever run before—way longer. Finally, I saw water ahead, but I didn't see safety boats. This meant we would not be swimming, and that knowledge helped me keep going.

Then when we made it to the water, boats suddenly appeared. I knew I was at my breaking point.

We got to the beach, and with no break, the instructors had us suit up and enter the water. I knew I couldn't go any further. I had no idea where we were swimming to because we had never left from that spot before and I couldn't see the other shore or anywhere to go. After the run we had just completed, I wouldn't have been surprised if they made us swim across the entire ocean!

I was so demoralized, and I no longer had any landmarks to help me set a goal. I couldn't see an end to the swim, and I started to go up and down in the swells as we headed farther into the open water away from shore.

I was done! This was the end, and I was ready to break when suddenly, I heard a whistle. I wasn't positive, so I looked around, and sure enough, someone had quit!

I knew there were only two of us left to quit, and I knew one would be me. But I figured I might as well be the last guy to quit instead of second-to-last. Then I heard another whistle, and I felt so happy. "My turn next!" I told myself.

I decided I would wait until the boat came by me again, as we had now separated from each other a bit and the boat was making large circles around the group of swimmers. I knew I was done! Every time my arm took a stroke and came close to the whistle, I felt like grabbing it and blowing.

I was certain that at any moment, I would actually follow through and quit. Then all of a sudden, I heard another whistle.

I was shocked. There were suddenly only six of us left!

Almost immediately, a loud horn sounded, and we were hauled from the water. The six of us just lay there exhausted.

The people who had quit were already in a separate boat, and they stayed there for the ride home. The difference between me and the last guy who quit was merely seconds.

Sometimes hanging on is just a matter of hanging on a bit longer than everyone else.

Our course ended on day nineteen, and I found out more about my character than I knew. As Booker T. Washington said, "Character is power."

PART TWO

Oath of Allegiance

When a brave man takes a stand, the spines of others are stiffened.
—Billy Graham

We never fail when we try to do our duty;
we only fail when we neglect to do it.
—Robert Baden Powell

STRENGTH FOUR

DUTY

"Success means doing the right thing no matter what."

I love the Dr. Seuss book *Horton Hatches the Egg*. It tells the story of an elephant named Horton who agrees to watch over an egg until its mother returns. He faces every possible reason not to stick with it, but he refuses to give up. He gave his word, and he does his agreed-upon duty no matter what challenges come. The thesis of the book is "An elephant's faithful, one hundred percent!"

Our world would be so much better if all of us approached duty this way. The real question for each of us is: Am I faithful, one hundred percent? And more to the point: Will I be faithful, one hundred percent, to my duty in the future?

Another question is: Should you name one of your children after Horton? I'm just kidding, but all of us should learn from Horton's example of duty.

A Great Debate

When a man or woman joins the military and reports to basic training, there is a clear assumption that duty may require sacrificing life for country. Why would anyone choose such a path?

Throughout history, there has been a great debate about whether duty should be based on love or punishment. Specifically, as the philosopher John Locke framed the question, should we do our duty because God will bless us, or because He'll punish us if we don't? Because it will win us worldly wealth and fame, or because it will bring the disrespect of others if we fail in our duties?[37]

I am a firm believer that love, not hope of reward or fear of bad consequences, is the real reason people do their duty. I learned this in the military, and I believe it holds true in other areas of life as well.

Socrates defined duty as a man doing what he ought to do and noted that all people are born with important duties that we should keep.[38] This idea, that man has inherent duties, is even more central to the founding of Western civilization than the concept of inalienable rights. In fact, the West was established by combining the great ideas of Jerusalem and Athens and their most famous martyrs, Jesus and Socrates.

The ideas of rights, freedom, justice, progress, leadership, and success that are central to Western civilization are rooted in the teachings and examples of these two men, both of whom died for what they believed. Jesus is the greatest example of duty because He chose to give His life for us. The most poignant expression of duty ever given is Jesus's exclamation to His Father, "Not My will, but Thine be done."[39]

> **Throughout history, many great men and women have given their lives to stand for what they believed.**

Socrates, though certainly a flawed man in many ways, felt it was his duty to ask questions of the leading people in Athens, to humble their pride and help them see the importance of justice and freedom. Even when he was given the choice to save his life by denying what he had been teaching, he felt it his duty to die rather than fail in what he believed was his life purpose.

Throughout history, many great men and women (from the martyrs of Rome to Joan of Arc and many others) have given their lives to stand for what they believed. And in the military, the idea of jeopardizing one's life and limb for the duty to others is a basic principle.

Duty in History

In his book *Duty, Honor, Country: A History of West Point*, historian Stephen Ambrose wrote that in European nations, nearly all military leaders came from the ruling aristocratic families.

The duty of military officers for many centuries was to their country, and very often, this meant a duty to the royal family or ruling party of the time.

In North America, in contrast, most military leaders were taught that their duty was to the nation itself. This shift was the natural result of the New World nations being established in the eighteenth and nineteenth centuries, an era that believed more in the power of the people than in the old values of the nobility.

The European idea of *noblesse oblige* (the obligation or duty of the nobility to take care of everyone else) was gradually replaced with the American Dream—the belief that everyone, no matter how humble, has a great role to play.

Growing up in Canada in the last quarter of the twentieth century, I witnessed a society where some people operated according to the old social class model, and at the same time, others believed that anyone could become great. For example, in the military, merit ruled, but politics was still always part of the culture.

Duty to What?

The great political thinker Montesquieu taught something very important about duty. He noted that the concept of duty means different things in different cultures. For example, in a nation actively ruled by a king or queen, duty means loyalty and service to the monarchy. But if the ruler is a tyrant or dictator, duty means loyalty and service to the one person in charge, not the monarchy as an institution.

In an aristocratic nation, duty usually means loyalty and service to the parliament or other legislative body that rules the nation, which is usually made up mostly of representatives from the various aristocratic families.

In a democratic republic, duty means loyalty and service to the constitution and people of the nation, specifically in regard to their freedom and protection. In addition to loyalty and service, duty also means dedication and being effective in your service. In the United States, for example, military leaders take an oath to defend the Constitution. That is where their duty lies.

In the Canadian military, the Oath of Allegiance combines these two traditions (aristocratic and democratic) by swearing to protect the monarchy and all its heirs and successors, according to law, which includes the monarchy as well as the government.

> **It is impossible to valiantly do one's duty without knowing what it is.**

In short, duty is always tied to loyalty, but different cultures have differing views on what or whom we should loyally serve. This is a very important point because it is impossible to valiantly do one's duty without knowing what it is.

A Canadian View

I have a slightly different view of duty than some people, and I'll say more about this in a minute. But first I want to help my non-Canadian readers understand something about the culture in which I was raised. Maybe humor will do this more effectively than anything else.

One of my favorite comedians is Jeff Foxworthy. He shared a whole segment on, "You know you're Canadian if...," and some of his jokes really hit home with me. For example, you know you're Canadian if...

- Your local Dairy Queen is closed from September to May.
- Someone in a Home Depot store offers you assistance, even though he or she doesn't work there.
- You have a lengthy conversation with someone when you dial the wrong number.
- Vacationing means going south of Detroit.
- You install security lights in your house and garage and then leave them both unlocked.
- You design your kid's Halloween costume to fit over a snowsuit.
- You wear shorts and a parka at the same time.

Actually, I've seen people wear shorts and parkas in Michigan as well. Foxworthy goes on and on, and all the jokes are pretty funny. The truth is I'm using this humor to hopefully soften you up because I'm going to share some rough boot-camp lessons in this chapter.

Two Internal Cultures

But I also have another reason beyond humor for sharing these jokes. As funny as these jokes are, they point out that there really are some interesting and at times comical differences between US and Canadian cultures. And if you've traveled to Britain or France or other places in the world, you know that cultures can be very different.

The two cultures we're going to cover in this chapter are even bigger than American, Western, European, or Asian cultures. In fact, all people in the world basically fall into one or the other. The first culture is what I call the culture of Convenience, and the other is the culture of Excellence.

Here's the thing: You can't fully serve convenience and excellence. You can't serve two masters. Oh, you can do a little of both, but ultimately, one of these cultures is going to rule your life. And you get to choose. But choose wisely because whichever culture you select will eventually determine your future.

You have to pick which one you want to dominate your life, and in making this choice, you actually decide your life path. In Canada, for example, we have to drive a lot to do most business. We can't be sissies about driving, any more than I could get through boot camp being a sissy about running and doing push-ups. Some things are simply necessary for success.

Excellence over Convenience

I once started a speech by saying, "If anyone here thinks you are a sissy bellyacher, please stand up right now." I guess I was expressing my inner military disciplinarian. Out of the thousands in the audience, only about thirty stood. I don't know if they were joking or serious, but I let them keep standing for most of the speech—just in case they needed to toughen up.

> **When we argue for our limitations, we get to keep them.**

But seriously, I love the fact that I grew up in difficult Canadian winters because they taught me to focus on excellence rather than be driven by convenience. Hard things can be such great blessings.

Unfortunately, when we argue for our limitations, we get to keep them. When we make lame excuses to ourselves, we tend to listen. This is taking the route of convenience, and it really does exclude us from true excellence. When we give in to our limitations, instead of trying to overcome them, we choose to be only partially excellent—which really isn't excellence at all.

My point is that each of us has internal battles between these two cultures, convenience and excellence. And we simply must choose excellence! This one choice will make all the difference in life. We have to choose excellence if we want to succeed in our life purpose. This means that we have to say no to a life focused on convenience.

In fact, I bet some of you are reading this all comfortable with your popcorn and chips and six-sugar Tim Horton's coffees. And you shouldn't be! Remember, you're at boot camp right now. So if you are too comfortable, get down on the ground right now and give me twenty push-ups. Then give me twenty more.

What Duty Really Means

I'm just kidding. But seriously, we need to choose excellence over convenience. We have to be willing to do the hard things that bring success! That's duty. Real duty is duty to your life purpose—to living your best life.

This is duty to God, family, and country—because when you are your best self, your truly excellent self, you serve God, family, and country at the highest level! This is real. Anything less than excellence means you aren't quite doing your duty.

George Eliot wrote, "It's a father's duty to give his sons a fine chance."[40] We have so many important duties to our families, our country, and God. For example, Hindu leader Swami Vivekananda said, "Devotion to duty is the highest form of worship of God." Our life purpose is the work God wants us to do in this world, and it is our duty to follow through. When we fail to do this, it's a huge tragedy, even if nobody ever notices.

Mortimer Adler, the editor of the *Great Books of the Western World*, said it very clearly: "Whatever is right to do we are obliged to do…in obedience to the commands of moral law."[41] The Roman emperor Marcus Aurelius, one of Rome's greatest generals, put it this way: "It is thy duty to order thy life well in every single act."

All of our choices (every little decision and action in our lives) create our internal culture—a set of beliefs, values, strengths, and duties. All of this builds momentum. And over time, this internal culture paces us, influences our decisions, and has a huge impact on what we think, say, do, and achieve.

> **All of our choices (every little decision and action in our lives) create our internal culture.**

We have to be careful and wise about this internal culture. We want it to help us, not distract or weaken us. For example, when we rationalize away our duties, when we make excuses for the sake of convenience over excellence, we add one more negative tweak to our internal culture.

But you know what's awesome? The opposite is also true. Every time we do the right thing for the right reason, even in minor affairs, we nudge our internal culture in the right direction. And it gets better and stronger over time. Each choice to do our real duty to our life purpose makes us just a little bit tougher, and over the days, weeks, months, years, and decades, we can become truly excellent. This is the path to real toughness.

Choosing excellence over convenience really strengthens us. I love the way my friend Orrin Woodward shows up at an airport, books a flight, sits in the worst seat at the back, and enjoys the trip by just reading a book the whole time. He ignores convenience and treats flying as simply what it is—a simple mode of transportation, a way of getting somewhere fast.

It's really quite a wonder to watch. He doesn't check in early, he happily sits in the middle seat for a long flight, and he doesn't give any thought to comfort. He spends a lot of his life traveling, reading books as he goes, ignoring convenience and just getting the job done.

If he could, I think he'd just live in a cabin and read books all day. But to live his purpose, he works his butt off helping people. He does very little for convenience, but he works like crazy to fulfill his life purpose.

Real Balance Means Choosing Excellence

Those who focus on comfort and convenience will never achieve such excellence. They'll never live up to their potential. Of course, I'm not saying you should never relax or that you should put sharp rocks or a bag of hammers under your sheets each night so that you'll toughen up—not at all. We need balance in our lives, times to have fun and enjoy. For example, I love my relaxed time with my family.

But often, people use the word *balance* as an excuse to avoid the hard work of success.

Those who succeed know that in addition to happy, relaxed times in life, we must also spend a good portion of our waking hours doing the things that bring excellence. It's our duty to our life purpose.

> Often, people use the word *balance* as an excuse to avoid the hard work of success.

I love how John F. Kennedy described duty: "A man does what he must—in spite of personal consequences, in spite of obstacles and dangers and pressures—and that is the basis of all human morality."[42]

Two Kinds of People

Another way to say this is that there are two kinds of people in this world: those who do what is convenient and wish they had the life they only dream of, and those who figure out their life purpose and do what it takes to achieve it—even when it's hard.

That's the world we live in. What you have to ask yourself is: Which type am I? And which type am I going to be from now on?

If you adopt the culture of convenience, you're going to let yourself and the rest of us down. If you choose the culture of excellence, in contrast, you'll put yourself on a path to a lot of happiness, success, and even greatness. It's a tough path, but this life was meant for tough people. We were born to do great things, and we all need to live up to our potential. This means choosing excellence over convenience, and sticking to this choice.

When others don't do their duty, they let us all down. Of course, it's not right for anyone else to make us do our life purpose, even though failing to do so will let everyone down. Each person must figure out and carry out his life purpose for himself. As US president Ronald Reagan once said, "Government's first duty is to protect the people, not run their lives." We would all be much better off if governments listened to this advice and did their duty.

The Attitude of Easy Always Disappoints

I'm not saying that building a successful career or business can't ever be easy. If you choose the right path for you, it will probably be easier than other career paths you might select—because success is always more fun than pretty much anything else.

But we can't always have the attitude of seeking easy, never-ending comfort and a life and internal culture of convenience. We can't live our lives always trying to do what's easy. That's a sure road to failure. We have to do excellent things, not be controlled by what's convenient. That's what I mean when I say we need to toughen up.

A Definition of Duty

And here's my view of duty: It's our duty to toughen up! It's our duty to choose excellence over convenience. It's our duty!

Maybe I'm saying this too strongly for some people, but this is how I really feel. Whatever your life is, it will almost surely require you to sweat and bleed a bit. The scars you acquire from the courage of taking the excellent path, the path of duty, will never make you feel inferior. Instead, they'll open doors to greater things. They'll give you confidence and strength and wisdom. They'll make you better and tougher.

> **It's our duty to toughen up! It's our duty to choose excellence over convenience. It's our duty!**

Sadly, many people are slaves to convenience. They don't accomplish all they can and should because they notice every possible inconvenience and use it as an excuse. There's really only one solution to this: It's time to toughen up. It's time to do our duty.

Let me say this as clearly as I know how: It is our duty to do our best, to live our deep life purpose, to live up to our potential. If we fall short of what we could have done in the world, for God and our families and our society, we let everyone down. Duty matters! Duty is essential.

As George MacDonald, the man whose writings convinced C. S. Lewis to become a believer, put it, "Until our duty becomes to us as common as breathing, we are poor creatures."[43] Without a life purpose and the duty it gives us, we are poor creatures indeed.

And remember this: Each of us is unique, and our life purpose is special to us. So when we fail to achieve our purpose, we leave the world forever worse off. Mark Batterson said, "Uniqueness isn't a virtue; it's a responsibility."[44] It's our duty.

Duty Is a Matter of Life and Death

As a military diver, my life depended on my buddies. If they hadn't done their duty, I literally would have died. I'd be dead right now. But they did their duty, and so I'm alive. The same is true about our life purpose. It may not be as immediate or obvious, but when a person fails in his duty and doesn't live up to his life purpose and potential, it hurts all of us.

We're all worse off because some people choose convenience over excellence in their lives. And we're all better off because some people have chosen to do their best, to live their life purpose to its fullest.

That's what it means to do our duty. George Washington said it clearly: "Human happiness and moral duty are inseparably connected."[45] Another American president, Theodore Roosevelt, predicted, "The things that will destroy America are prosperity at any price, safety first instead of duty first, and love of soft living…"

I love a story about hockey player Paul Kariya and how he refused to take the soft, easy way. During the 2003 Stanley Cup finals, Kariya took a huge blow that would have put most people out of the match. As the *Calgary Herald* newspaper reported it:

> Paul Kariya had his head down outside the blueline. Scott Stevens lined up and put him down.
>
> Lights out. Good night.
>
> See you next season.
>
> Rubber legged, taken to the dressing room, presumed done for the duration, Kariya got up, back in the game and scored the goal of goals to send the Anaheim Mighty Ducks to a 5-2 win and a seventh game of the Stanley Cup finals….
>
> "It woke me up," Kariya laughed….

He didn't have a point in the first four games and only a second assist in the nine goal night which was Game 5.

But here in Game 6 last night, Kariya—who also had two assists—scored his first goal of the final series....It goes down as one of the most dramatic moments in Stanley Cup finals history.[46]

Kariya's coach, Mike Babcock, said:

He was courageous....Anytime that happens, it's a big message to your team about leadership. It was a great way to respond. I was impressed by that. It was impressive for him. I think he's got to feel good about it.

When you are stretched and people are calling you out and when you respond like that...that's the best feeling.[47]

Kariya wasn't just tough; he also used his toughness to do his duty for his team. He went beyond the minimum and really gave his all.

Note that duty goes beyond personal relationships and influences whole nations and societies. As Jonathan Sacks put it, "Those who believe that liberal democracy and the free market can be defended by the force of law and regulation alone, without an internalized sense of duty and morality, are tragically mistaken."

Knowledge, Confidence, and Action

Now I want to share two important suggestions on *how* to do our duty more effectively. First, knowledge is a vital part of duty. Here's the formula: Knowledge equals information repeated. So when we repeat true information, our knowledge increases. And increased knowledge boosts confidence. Confidence brings action. And the right actions bring results.

In other words, we need to know our life purpose and then live it. It really is that simple. We have to strive for it, work for it, and settle for nothing less than real excellence. Never let convenience or any other distraction get in the way. That's toughness. And it's our duty.

Think of the world as a whole right now. Do we need leaders, or do we need timid people? Should we be sissies and wimps, or do we need to stand up like men and women of greatness? Our whole society needs better leadership, in our homes, families, businesses, governments, and institutions. And better leadership comes from people who know their life purpose and consistently choose excellence over convenience.

Hesitancy versus Strength

When we don't know our purpose, we don't know our duty—and we can't do it. People who aren't clear about their life purpose feel confused and in doubt. This creates hesitancy and inaction.

But when we know our purpose, we know our duty. And then we just have to live that duty by choosing excellence and never lowering the bar. Abraham Lincoln wisely counseled, "Let us have faith that right makes might; and in that faith let us, to the end, dare to do our duty as we understand it."[48] General George S. Patton said it even more directly, in typical military language: "Do your duty as you see it, and damn the consequences."[49]

Success is really very simple, after all. It isn't easy, but it's simple. We just have to know our duty and live up to it. This is hard work. It kicks our butts. But it is the road to leadership and success, and all of us need to toughen up and take it.

A Plan

Second, part of living our duty is having a good plan. Plans make a huge difference in whether we fail or succeed. For example, imagine you're building a house and the contractor says, "I don't think we need blueprints. I mean, we've got the lumber and the tools, right? So let's just start digging and hammering and piece it together as we go. Don't waste any money on planning."

How quickly will you be looking for another contractor?

Or you're playing a football game, you go back to the huddle, and the quarterback says, "I have no idea what play we should run. Just hike the ball, and let's see what happens. I mean, I just don't know what to do...."

> **Part of living our duty is having a good plan.**

Uh, your team isn't going to win many games on this model. Plans matter.

Or maybe your military unit is under fire in some place like Afghanistan, Iraq, or Somalia, and your leader says, "I don't know what to do! I...I...Oh no! They're shooting. What should we do?"

You're in a bad spot there. No leadership, no success. No plan, no leadership. Good leaders make plans and execute them. They are flexible and adjust plans as needed to succeed, but they do the work to wisely think things through and really plan. This is a part of doing our duty, and a good plan helps us clearly know and do our duty.

Without a plan, duty is unclear, and confusion too often wins the day. So to get your duty clear and help others do their duties, make a good plan.

Plans also help us put our life purpose on paper. They help make it real. Once a plan is clear, it helps everyone involved. It helps us work together because a shared plan is powerful.

A good plan also creates confidence. So get a plan. Take the time to make it a good plan. Infuse your duty into the plan, and make sure it will demand your very best and inspire you—and others—to excellence. Don't let convenience ruin your plan. Find out what is needed and what will best achieve it, and then get to work.

Focus Counts

Good plans create focus. One of the things that make basic training so effective is the plan. The routine, the schedule, the clear requirements and duties—all of these combine to take regular people from many walks of life and turn them into effective soldiers and sailors. Those who don't meet the standards established by the plan wash out. The plan gets results.

As a leader, it is essential for you to put together the right plan. When the right plan is in place, doing your duty, toughening up, and achieving real excellence are just the natural consequences of implementing and sticking to the plan.

Few people ever succeed above the level of their plan. So make your plan, hold it to the right standard, and then stick to it (and adjust it as needed) until you've achieved your highest goals and purpose. Make it a truly excellent plan, and then, whatever happens, just toughen up and keep going.

Duty Is Power

In addition to all these things, perhaps the most important thing about duty is that it gives us a compass, a map, a ruler by which to judge our lives. As the philosopher Immanuel Kant said, "An action, to have moral worth, must be done from duty." And in the words of TV personality Ben Stein: "I came to realize that life lived to help others is the only one that matters and that is my duty.... This is my highest and best use as a human."[50]

When we clearly understand our life purpose, and have a wisely considered plan for achieving it, it naturally fills us with confidence and infuses us with excitement and motivation to do our very best.

When this requires us to do hard things, our resolve and toughness are tested. Will we stand up and do the right thing, or will we give in to convenience? Helen Keller addressed this difficult choice when she said, "One painful duty fulfilled makes the next plainer and easier." When we do our duty today, it is easier to do it tomorrow.

More on Duty in History

The ancient Roman Empire conquered much of Europe, the Middle East, and northern Africa, and many historians believe their success was based mostly on the strength of their armies. The glue that held the Roman armies together was what they called *officium*, which is directly translated into English as "duty."

Many cultures throughout history have emphasized duty much more than our modern democracies tend to. For example, just like citizens of Rome, every young citizen in many nations, from Israel to Spain and beyond, is required to serve in the military as a duty to his or her nation. Other countries teach duty to society as part of every young person's education.

Sadly, many free nations have stopped teaching or demanding serious duties from citizens. In Canada and the United States, for example, many people think that if they vote, they've basically done their duty to their country. Yet our duty to pass more freedom than we inherited to

> Sadly, many free nations have stopped teaching or demanding serious duties from citizens.

our children and grandchildren is often ignored. As a result, we tend to fail in such duties.

Adler wrote that citizens have at least three overarching duties, which can be characterized as "cares, functions, and loyalties." Voting is a function, as is jury duty or simply obeying the laws of your nation. Cares and loyalties are more complex, and we all have a duty to care about the right things as citizens and to maintain the right loyalties.

Beyond the role of citizen, we also have duties of function, cares, and loyalties in our marriage, family, career, and business. These all carry important responsibilities, and how we live up to them largely determines what kind of leaders we become and how much success we obtain. We need to be like Horton and follow the wise maxim, "An elephant's faithful, one hundred percent."[51] Sadly, this isn't widely taught or emphasized in society.

Duty and Success

To turn this around, we need a wholesale return to the concept of duty. We need to talk about it more and do more to serve others. Most of all, we need to know our life purpose, understand that it is our duty to achieve it (and all its functions, cares, and loyalties), and then let nothing stop us in this great endeavor. Duty matters, and our generation needs to do our duty at a much higher level.

Next to having the right attitude, living with courage, and building solid character, finding and faithfully fulfilling our duty constitutes one of the most important strengths of genuine leaders and truly successful people.

War is the greatest evil Satan has invented to corrupt
our hearts and souls. We should honor our soldiers,
but we should never honor war.
—Dean Hughes

STRENGTH FIVE

HONOR

"Be the kind of person who always honors those who deserve it."

So far, we've discussed four of the Eight Strengths of great leadership and success, and as you can tell by now, all of them fit together. As we grow in one of these strengths, it frequently helps us improve in the others. The Fifth Strength is no exception. In fact, honor increases our effectiveness in all of the other strengths.

Honor is terribly important. As Abraham Lincoln put it, "I am not bound to win, but I am bound to be true. I am not bound to succeed, but I am bound to live up to what light I have." And as Plato said, "You should not honor men more than truth."

Without honor, nothing else really matters in our lives. George Bernard Shaw wrote, "The most tragic thing in the world is a man of genius who is not a man of honor."

One of my favorite quotes about honor comes from an unlikely source, Machiavelli, who said, "It is not titles that honor men, but men that honor titles." This gets to the heart of what honor is all about. Honor is at the core of good leadership.

What Does Honor Really Mean?

On a personal note, sometimes life surprises us. As our business grew, I realized more and more how important it was that I could learn from those who had gone before me.

Too often people think they can become leaders and obtain success on their own. After all the hard work of building our business, it's almost impossible for me to describe how grateful we felt to those who helped us and showed us the way.

For example, imagine how crazy scary it must have been for Christopher Columbus. He thought he was right, but can you imagine how it must have felt to climb onto the boat and head off into deep water?

Taking risks is hard. It takes courage, it takes work, and it takes a true spirit of initiative and innovation. But all great progress comes from such risk.

Think about it. We don't really care who came after Columbus because everyone who came later had a map, well, maybe not literally. But they had the benefit of someone having already shown them the way. Columbus had faith with no evidence. He went on a hunch. The rest of them didn't need faith because he had already shown them what to do.

By definition, Columbus was the leader, and the rest were followers.

It took real faith to just sail into the unknown seas, and that is worthy of a lot of respect and honor. I honor Columbus for taking this risk and setting this example of initiative and leadership.

That's right: honor. In the military, we speak of duty, honor, and courage, or sometimes duty, honor, and country. And in history, honor has often been used to mean almost the same thing as duty or even character.

The modern English word *duty* originally came from the Latin word *debutus*, which meant "to owe," while the word *honor* came from the Latin *honorem*, which meant dignity, reputation, chastity, virtue, courtesy, and distinction.[52]

Mortimer Adler explained the difference between duty and honor this way: "Duty usually involves obligations to others, but a man's sense of honor may lead him to act in a certain way though the good of no other is involved. To maintain his self-respect he must respect a standard of conduct which he has set for himself."[53]

Duty is what we owe to others; honor refers to our internal standards of our best potential. Adler also notes that while many people may have fame or notoriety, honor is reserved for those who truly deserve to be *known* and emulated.[54] Homer taught that honor is a significant motivation for real heroes.[55]

The American founding fathers, at least the ones who signed the Declaration of Independence, considered honor to be sacred. This is why they pledged their lives, their fortunes, and their "sacred honor" to the cause of freedom. In truth, when we live with honor, we treat our whole approach to life as deeply sacred. We see our work and our service as special.

As a Canadian, I understand this concept as expressed by John Diefenbaker in the July 1, 1960, Canadian Bill of Rights: "I am a Canadian, free to speak without fear, free to worship in my own way, free to stand for what I think is right, free to oppose what I believe to be wrong, or free to choose those who shall govern my country. This heritage of freedom I pledge to uphold by myself and all mankind." It is an honor to defend and stand up for this kind of freedom.

Another Canadian, Lester Pearson, once wrote, "As we enter our centennial year we are still a young nation, very much in the formative stages. Our national condition is still flexible enough that we can make almost anything we wish with our nation. No other country is in a better position than Canada to go ahead with the evolution of a national purpose devoted to all that is good and noble and excellent in the human spirit."

I love Pearson's use of the word *noble*. Living with honor is the way to live nobly. And while it is our *duty* to stand up for and maintain our freedoms, it is also our *honor* to do so, and it is our honor to do whatever else we can to improve our families, our communities, and our society.

And as Pearson put it, it is our honor to always strive for excellence. Nothing less is worthy of our honor. Some people honor their video games or TV more than their potential for real excellence. That's sad. I know a lot people in their thirties who spend more time playing video games than they do with their kids.

I love the following letter to the editor that I read years ago in the newspaper, titled "Unsuper Mario":

> You're 31 years old, stop playing video games. You don't have a job, you neglect your girlfriend (my sister) and, more importantly, your son. Be a man, take care of your responsibilities. Why is it today's males still act like children? Your grandfather, who you brag about fighting the Germans in Holland, did so at the age of 20. He wasn't sitting on his ass getting fat off chips, pop and playing *Call of Duty*. —A Very Unhappy Sister

When I read that at seminars, it usually gets a standing ovation. Honor matters.

The *Oxford English Dictionary* also defines *duty* and *honor* a bit differently, and the nuances are really interesting. For example, while *duty* is defined as "something one has to do because it is morally right or legally necessary,"[56] a kind of debt to society (in fact, in some places the word *duty* is used interchangeably with *tax* or *tariff*), *honor* is defined as (1) "great respect," (2) "a clear sense of what is morally right," and (3) "something that is a privilege and a pleasure."[57]

I really like these differences. While the second definition of honor listed here is pretty much the same thing as duty, the other two definitions teach us something very important. Honor is something that is "a privilege and a pleasure," and it is also used to pay "great respect" to people who are worthy of being honored.

One of the best ways to understand this is to consider another definition from the *Oxford English Dictionary*, which says that duty is something "done because of a feeling of obligation rather than enthusiasm."[58]

Honor, on the other hand, is all about enthusiasm! When we have honor, we do the right things because we really, truly feel passionate about them. We don't necessarily *have* to do them to be a good person, like we do with our duties, but we *choose* to do them because we care.

This is what it means to live with honor. And living honorably, not because we owe it to anyone but because we choose it, is the attitude of real success. Those who have this attitude will do great things in life.

Moreover, when we approach life this way, we naturally honor the right people because we are deeply, profoundly grateful to them for their example, service, and sacrifices.

Gratitude

As Lana and I started experiencing real success, we felt overwhelming gratitude for Orrin and Laurie Woodward and the others who showed us the way. We felt great respect and a profound sense of honor toward them. We knew we simply could not have accomplished what we did without their help.

Earlier, we talked about the parts of honor that are most like duty. But while the "great respect" element of honor is understood by many in the military, I don't think it is clearly understood by enough civilians.

In the military, we care a lot about honoring those who went before us, who set the example of excellence, hard work, and loyalty, and who paid the ultimate sacrifice with their lives. We honor them whenever we can.

We are awarded medals that are named after and honor past accomplishments of ordinary soldiers and sailors who have done extraordinary things, and we often wear patches and other signs of respect and admiration for what past men and women have accomplished.

We learn about the successes and failures of great examples and heroes who have gone before us, and we try to give honor where honor is due.

Never Forget!

To me, this kind of honor is very important, yet it is often missing in business and family. That's sad. And in a way, it's disrespectful. We need to honor those who paved the way for our opportunities and success.

We should never forget the sacrifices of others, and we should take every opportunity to honor those who have earned our respect and helped us succeed. This is crucially important.

For example, the sacrifices of people such as Orrin Woodward and Chris Brady to make my business possible bring out my eternal gratitude. I am so thankful to them.

I honor them. That doesn't mean I think they are perfect, but it does mean that I'll go out of my way to show them how much I respect and love them. I felt the same way about some of my military leaders.

> **Great leaders understand that we need to give honor to those who deserve it.**

Great leaders understand that we need to give honor to those who deserve it. And over the years, I've learned that the most important way to honor them is to stay humble, keep learning from them, and apply what they teach us. I've learned many of my most important life lessons from these heroes and role models.

In that spirit, I want to honor them by sharing some of the top things they've taught me. The great English cleric Charles Colton said that "imitation is the highest form of flattery," but I think the saying should be "Emulation is the highest form of honor." In fact, I think this second phrase is more in keeping with what Colton probably meant.

> **Emulation isn't imitation. It means learning the best lessons from someone and then applying them in our own unique way.**

Emulation isn't imitation. It means learning the best lessons from someone and then applying them in our own unique way. And honor is much more than flattery because it flows from love and true gratitude for a worthy and heroic example.

Here then are some of the top lessons I learned from my closest mentors and heroes. Lana and I have learned so much from them that this list is just a sample. But every item on this list is truly essential to real leadership and success.

Lesson One: Be Strong

Life will throw you challenges. Be strong. Life won't always be fair. Be strong anyway. Success comes to those who toughen up and make success more important than whatever is holding them back.

This bears repeating, just in case it didn't make the impression it should have the first time: Success comes to those who toughen up and make success more important than whatever is holding them back. So be strong.

Winners win. That's why we call them winners. People follow those who always find a way to overcome the odds.

I honor the strong leaders in my life, especially in business, who have shown me how to do this even in the face of painful difficulties.

Lesson Two: Give Up Some Stuff

Just say no to some things in your life so you can focus on the really important things. You'll probably see your success increase as you do this. For example, when Lana and I achieved the highest level of our business, we started getting asked to speak every week.

People who do this get paid a lot in speaker fees, so speaking weekly really sets them up financially. The downside is that, in many cases, they neglect their day-to-day responsibilities, and their business goes backward.

We resolved to speak only once a month, and though this brought in a lot less money during the year, we were able to really work on our business and build for the long term. Years later, our business is much stronger than it would have been had we chosen the short-term approach.

Giving up things that don't matter much for those that really matter is a quick way to improve your life. Jettison anything that takes you away from your major calling.

Focus is the ability to give up good opportunities so you can have the best. Sometimes your success is determined by what you are willing to ignore.

I honor the mentors who have taught me by their example how to always keep my priorities in place.

Lesson Three: Toughen Up to Criticism

In the military, I heard, "If you want to sacrifice the admiration of many men for the criticism of a few, go ahead." Too often people let the criticism of a few hold them back from doing great things. We all need to be a little harder in the helmet.

For example, I don't know how true this story is, but I heard of a cancer clinic that came up with a treatment for pancreatic cancer that extended a person's life span by twelve to twenty-four months. Think of it! Pancreatic cancer is among the deadliest forms of cancer and one of the quickest killers. It often kills people in six months or less. But this was a simple, natural treatment that was easy to administer.

The treatment was doing a coffee enema, and it was so successful that the doctors decided to send their patients home to be with their friends and loved ones. After all, they could do the treatment on their own.

> **We all need to be a little harder in the helmet.**

But when the people went home with their families, the results were terrible. The doctors didn't know why the treatment worked so well in the clinic but so poorly at home. In response, the researchers sent the next round of patients home with journals to record their treatments along with their thoughts and feelings.

The journals showed that the patients' friends and families criticized and ridiculed the coffee enemas so strongly that the patients would simply stop doing the treatments. I can just imagine the brother-in-law saying, "Hey, Joe, you want cream with your coffee?"

This is a really sad story. These people ended up dying sooner just because they listened to criticism.

> **I will always be grateful to the example of leaders who took unfair and often extreme criticism and just kept doing the right thing anyway.**

Leaders learn to ignore unfair or unmerited criticism; otherwise, they'll never succeed. I've always been amazed at the grace with which Orrin Woodward handles criticism and keeps his Christian attitude. He never lets it sway him from doing what he feels is right.

I will always be grateful to the example of leaders who took unfair and often extreme criticism and just kept doing the right thing anyway.

I honor them for this.

Lesson Four: Don't Be So Easily Offended or Sensitive

Let your boss or spouse say something negative or potentially hurtful and just let it roll off your back. Don't spend energy on the junk. Give grace easily, and focus on what matters instead of being pulled into hurt or arguments.

Leadership isn't for little boys or girls, after all; it's for real men and women. Don't get distracted by offenses when you can just let them go and move on.

It takes a big person to do this, but it will help you on your path to greatness.

Master your emotions, or they will master you. Remember that hurting people are those who hurt others, so when someone hurts you, try to understand that he or she is hurting. Getting offended is a choice. As my friend and business partner Raylene MacNamara often says, "You have to have thick skin and a soft heart, not thin skin and a hard heart."

I honor the mentors who have shown this profound example.

Lesson Five: Don't Get Discouraged

In many years of working with people, both in the military and in business, I have learned that more often than not, the thing that keeps people from success is discouragement about their current situation—whatever it is.

Don't waste your life or time being discouraged. Just forget it, and go do something that really matters. Building something important is a pretty sure way to end or at least ignore the effects of discouragement.

My friend Wayne MacNamara never gets discouraged, or at least he never shows it. He is an eternal optimist, and this is a great example to me. Wayne was a competitive bodybuilder for many years, and no matter what happens, he focuses on the positive. Those who work with him always want to be around him because his sunny attitude turns everything to success. He has shown me how being positive is a true part of toughness.

I honor those who put aside discouragement and just keep working—positively, productively, and with smiles on their faces.

Lesson Six: Track Your Time and Money

We track what we respect. If you don't respect your money, you won't track it. If you do respect your time, you'll track it. This is really simple.

For example, has anyone ever told you that he just doesn't have time to do some important project? Through the years, I've noticed that the busiest people are the best ones to put in charge of something because they track their time and will make it happen. Those who don't respect their time and money enough to track them are always too busy and broke.

Part of tracking your money is just being smart about it. My friend Joce Dionne is so good with money because he always tracks it closely. As he often says, "If you're not a tightwad, you won't have a wad."

Respect your time and money. For example, we could shut down

> We track what we respect. If you don't respect your money, you won't track it. If you do respect your time, you'll track it.

your city tonight just by having everyone who owns this book tweet to everyone they know in town that gas prices will go way up tomorrow. A lot of people will get up and drive to the gas station and wait in a line of ten cars—all idling. A whole row of rocket scientists!

That's funny. They'll spend five dollars to drive across town and save twenty dollars in the fill-up. Then they'll spend fifteen dollars on snacks or burgers before they drive home.

Instead, you want to be one of those who tracks your finances and thinks things through. I recommend reading and applying an excellent book on personal finance, *Financial Fitness*, with an introduction by Orrin Woodward and Chris Brady. It is full of the lessons I learned about finances from my mentors and through personal experience.

I honor those who have shown and taught me to respect and track the things that are important resources in achieving my goals and life purpose.

Lesson Seven: Focus on the Next Thing

If you ever get in a rut, stop trying to do everything. Instead, focus on the next problem or opportunity on your plate. Do the next thing, do it well, and let the rest take care of itself. Then repeat this process.

Usually, it's only one thing that's holding you back. Your mentor often knows what the one thing is, even if you don't. So identify the top one next thing on your plate, and fix or fulfill it.

This is really powerful and effective advice.

Keep your head in the game by keeping the game in your head. When Lana and I were working to reach the highest level of our business, we would tell our mentor, "Three months from now when we see you again, we'll hit the goal." Then, the next time we were together, I'd tell him the same thing.

Finally, he said, "You keep saying that, but it never happens. How can you keep saying that?" But for me, that was the next goal, so I just stayed focused on it until I reached it. I knew I had to keep my focus.

I honor those who taught me this principle and showed me how to do it.

Lesson Eight: Add Value First

This is a law of prosperity and success: We must add value for others before we expect to receive or benefit ourselves. Stephen Covey taught that we should "seek first to understand, then to be understood."[59] On an even bigger scale, successful leaders learn to seek first to serve, help, and benefit people, and then the benefits naturally come.

> **We must add value for others before we expect to receive or benefit ourselves.**

If you aren't loyal to the few, you won't be blessed with the many. You have to do the right things when you serve two people, or you won't ever get the chance to serve hundreds.

I honor the business partners and friends who have taught me this lesson, like my friend Dave, who kept coming to our meetings for a long time even though I wasn't producing much.

Lesson Nine: Remember That Initiative Must Come Before Evidence

In the early days of building our business, sometimes people would say to me, "Claude, I'll wait and see how you do. If you succeed, then I'll get involved." But in all the years I've been in business, and with all

> **Initiative always precedes evidence. Otherwise, it isn't really initiative.**

the success I've had, I've never had one of those people come back and do it—not one!

The reason is that they had the wrong mind-set. They wanted evidence to come before initiative, but if you've got all the evidence, you don't really need initiative. They needed to get their mind in the right place.

After all, which comes first? The right thinking or the results? The wood or the fire? Somebody who wants the fire before the wood is trying to put a 4 x 4 idea into a 2 x 2 mind. It just won't work. Initiative always precedes evidence. Otherwise, it isn't really initiative.

Successful people get their thinking in the right mode. And once people's minds stretch, it's almost impossible to go back. So keep sharing information, and help people think bigger. (Doesn't it feel great when you know more than your brother-in-law? That's one of the real pleasures in life.)

Sadly, people who want evidence in order to have faith or take initiative usually fail in most aspects of their lives.

I am so grateful to the people who taught me to take initiative and *then* watch for the evidence. I honor them for this. They have been a great blessing in my life.

Lesson Ten: Keep Your Will to Win

I love an old poem of sorts that I read entitled "Robbed." I'm not sure who wrote it, but here is how it goes:

> The dangerous people are not the ones
> Who hit you with clubs and rob you with guns.
> The thief will not attack your character traits
> Or belittle your abilities to your face.
> It will likely be a well-meaning friend
> Who merely crushes your will to win.

No, he doesn't rob you at the point of a gun.
He simply says it can't be done.
When you point to thousands who already are,
He smiles and says, "They're superior by far.
In personality, skills and abilities too,
They are way ahead of what you can do."

It matters not that their reasoning is wrong.
And their words untrue,
For you feel others must surely know you.
So you're robbed of your dreams and your hopes to succeed,
Robbed of material blessings you could have received.
Robbed of the faith that says "I can,"
Robbed by an ignorant, gunless friend.

So the deadliest of men is not he with a gun,
But the one who says, "It can't be done."
For that taken by burglars can be gotten again,
But what can replace your will to win?

Another Perspective on Honor

So far, we have discussed two kinds of honor: the honor of doing your duty and possessing character and integrity *and* the importance of honoring those who merit it—not only out of gratitude but also because it is the honorable thing to do and makes those who do it better people.

There is also a third kind of honor: the idea that is expressed by the phrase "I had to defend his honor." This concept is based on the belief that some things are worth fighting for, or more accurately, that some things simply *must* be fought for. This is an important principle.

At its most basic level, this idea defines honor as the necessity of making things right. In his book *Honor: A History*, James Bowman teaches that when a child is hit by a snowball or punched in the face by another child, almost anywhere around the globe, he will almost always respond with the view that he is honor-bound to hit back—to even things up and make things right. [60]

The strength of this feeling increases when an older sibling watches a younger sibling get hit or hurt, even more if a boy hits a smaller girl, and it reaches its peak if, for example, a bigger, stronger boy hits a small, disabled person in a wheelchair.

There is honor in righting such wrongs, according to most people, and many people believe that a failure to right such a wrong is itself either shameful or downright wrong. As Edmund Burke famously said, "All that is necessary for the triumph of evil is that good men do nothing."

I could say a lot more about this kind of honor and how it is often taken to extremes or used as an excuse to justify greedy or selfish behavior. But with that said, there are real rights and wrongs in the world, and part of leadership is taking a stand for what is honorable.

Those who stand by and let bad things happen on their watch can't really consider themselves successful or good leaders.

Not on Our Watch!

This is true in our political involvement as citizens, as well as in our roles as husbands and wives, as parents, and as human beings in general. It is also true in business. Good leaders take action to right wrongs in their stewardship. For example, if our generation allows our freedoms to be lessened, we will have participated in a dishonorable act.

We have to stand up and stop this from happening. As my friend Orrin Woodward puts it, "We can't let our freedoms decline—not on our watch!" We must do our best to maintain a free society.

Likewise, the current attack on entrepreneurial opportunity is a huge injustice, and anyone who cares about real freedom needs to do the honorable thing. Whatever we can do to spread and support entrepreneurship helps right the wrong of decreased economic opportunity for everyone.

The right to own and build your own business is under siege in many nations, and it is worth standing up for. The most effective way to win this battle is simply to be entrepreneurially successful and help others do the same. The more we do this, the better.

There is honor in any worthy work, and there is a special honor that comes from ownership, building things, and adding as much value as possible to society. The freedom to be an entrepreneur has afforded me an amazing lifestyle, not only in material things but also in family and life.

Ownership and the Return on Investment

As you can tell by now, I'm convinced that few things bring as much positive return on investment as owning and building a successful business. To succeed, businesses must offer a product or service that helps people over time and at a price they welcome. Businesses that last do so because they add real value to the lives of others, and businesses that don't do that fail.

In addition, businesses that also offer increased economic opportunity for widespread ownership naturally provide even more value to society.

It is interesting that on one occasion, a man I was meeting with used this exact language to tell me he didn't want to do the business. He said, "Claude, I just don't know if your work is a good return on investment."

I was shocked, and I replied, "Me? Are you kidding? You've been working in your job for thirty years! Thirty years! And you're still just barely paying the bills. That's a terrible return on investment. I mean, thirty years! Seriously? I feel so bad for you that I want to call your family together and have an intervention!

"I was broke for five years, but now I'm financially independent. That's a pretty great return on investment, don't you think? I say that humbly. But in this case, let's get real. I thought five years of barely scraping by was bad. I was miserable for most of it. I can't even imagine how you must feel after thirty years."

The sad thing is that thousands of people, actually millions, are in the same boat. They work their butts off for other people, and decades later, they're still living paycheck to paycheck. In a way, they're slaves to their jobs.

And they deserve something better, or many of them do. Now that's worth fighting for. And it's part of my life purpose to do something about it. I feel honor-bound to right this wrong.

> We need a world where people's hard work really helps their family, and the only thing that will ever accomplish this on a broad scale is entrepreneurship.

So many families suffer needlessly in this system, and you know what? I've dedicated my life to doing something about it. And I am. And I love it.

For me, it started out because I just wanted something better for my family. And over time, I discovered other reasons for building our business. But part of it is just plain honor. We need a world where people's hard work really helps their family, and the only thing that will ever accomplish this on the broad scale is entrepreneurship.

I respect that other people have different life purposes. But this is mine, and I'm going to keep doing it until they haul me off the stage kicking and screaming. Economic opportunity and independent business ownership are matters of honor worth fighting for. I've watched some of my closest friends lose almost everything fighting for this pursuit, and I'm going to keep standing for it for the rest of my life.

I hope you feel just as passionately about your life purpose. If so, I honor you for the path you're following. The future of the world depends on leaders who give their all for things that really matter. That's what honor is all about.

No road is long with good company.
—Turkish proverb

STRENGTH SIX

RELATIONSHIPS

**"Let them see me cry. It's okay.
I cry sometimes when I cuddle my son.
I'm soft with him and tough about
pursuing my life purpose."**

When Lana and I first started our business, we were at a big training seminar, and they announced that at the next month's meeting, they were going to have a Kenny Rogers impersonator come and perform. I was such a nerd I didn't know who Kenny Rogers was, and I didn't notice that they said "impersonator." So I assumed he was someone who had been successful in building a business or something like that.

A few days later, I was out building my business, and I wanted to sell ten tickets to the next month's event. Well, just in passing, I mentioned that they had Kenny Rogers coming, and the people perked right up and asked, "Kenny Rogers is in this?"

I said, "Yeah." They immediately signed up, so I kept mentioning the "Kenny Rogers" event. Pretty soon, I had around sixty people coming to the next meeting, instead of eking out our usual four or five.

I'm sharing this story because of what happened next. I had about sixty people who came to see Kenny Rogers, and when the look-alike came out on stage, he was the skinniest Kenny Rogers ever. He looked more like Kenny Loggins.

All these Kenny Rogers fans started getting up and leaving, and I stood up and tried to talk them into staying. "What's wrong?" I asked them. A bunch of them left, mad that I had misled them—even though it was an honest mistake.

Fortunately, one of our business leaders, Dave, saw that I had sold sixty tickets to this event and decided to fly out the next month to meet me and help me build my business. Sadly, the next month, we were down to the normal four tickets, but Dave had already booked his ticket, so he decided to honor his commitment and come anyway.

A Surprising Occurrence

I don't know why he did this, but he started coming to help me every month. This was surprising because I didn't have the numbers to justify his attention. But he did it anyway. And he kept coming, month after month. Never once did he tell me I was on my own or that I needed to do better before he could help me.

After three years of me not having much success, his colleagues asked him why on earth he kept helping me. But one day, Dave was playing golf with one of his mentors, and he said, "I've been going to see this kid—it's been three and a half years now—and he's had very little success. I think he's good, though. He does all the work."

His mentor asked, "How much have you spent going there to help him?"

He responded, "Over thirty-five thousand dollars."

And the mentor said, "Well, if you stop going now, you've lost it all."

A Change in Plans

So he came down again, and after the meeting, he did something different. Always before, he had booked the ticket for the next month right there at my house, but this time, he said, "Claude, I think you should come up to Edmonton this time for the major convention."

It was September, and the big event in Edmonton was in October. Dave left. Then Lana went out to sea for her navy job for several months, and I was sitting alone at home. I thought, "Well, Dave isn't coming back. He's helped me for almost four years, and I haven't helped him much at all. Now it's over, and I gave him pretty much nothing for all his effort."

> **Something just snapped....I put on my...jacket and combat boots... and I walked to the highway and started hitchhiking.**

I was feeling like I had really let him down. I had such a great opportunity to benefit from his help, and I just hadn't done my part. I wallowed for a while. It was a pretty sad feeling.

Then something just snapped. I immediately quit my military team, which required a demanding daily training schedule, and I took a simpler military job that gave me more free time.

Monday morning, I put on my search-and-rescue jacket and combat boots, stashed three samples of the vitamins and other products I sold for my business into my pack, and put a pistol in my belt, and I walked to the highway and started hitchhiking.

It was fine at first, and I made good time. Then I got bogged down in Pembroke, Ontario. It was cold, I had no food or money with me, and it was really miserable. I wondered why on earth I was doing this. I left the main highway and hiked to town. I decided to head back home, to give up.

Then I checked my messages. I had received a routine call from another leader in the business. It was just a quick message, from a guy I had never met, reminding me of the Edmonton event and telling me he'd pick me up at the airport if I needed a ride. His call was so positive and upbeat that I reconsidered my plan to quit. He said he was excited to meet me, and his message really got me excited again.

I'd gotten the same kind of call a lot of times, but this time, I was actually trying to get to the meeting. It was a shot in the arm for me, so I headed back out onto the highway and starting walking toward Edmonton all over again. I got picked up by an eighteen-wheeler, and we made good time.

I liked this first ride in a truck because the driver was a good guy who logged all his stops, wore the company uniform, and seemed very conscientious about his job. Later, I got picked up by another kind of truck driver. This one kept two sets of books, never obeyed the speed limit, and popped all kinds of pills while he drove.

Somewhere along the miles, I fell asleep. When I woke up, he had a bottle of my vitamin samples from my pack, and he was downing them with a big smile on his face. "These vitamins are the best uppers I've ever had," he said.

I thought that was really funny. "I'll sell you the whole box if you want," I told him.

"How much?"

"Fifty bucks," I said.

"Tell you what," he bargained. "I'll give you thirty bucks and two boxes of these ice cream bars I'm hauling in the back of the truck."

I replied, "You've got a deal if you stop the truck right now." I was so hungry, I couldn't wait for the next stop to eat that ice cream.

The Elevator Ride

When we got to Edmonton an hour later, he pulled his eighteen-wheeler right up to the front door of the fancy hotel hosting the business meeting. I got out, and I headed for the event.

I hadn't had a shower in several days, pretty much the only thing I'd eaten in days was the two boxes of ice cream bars, and to top it off, I had a splitting brainfreeze headache from the ice cream. But I walked into the lobby, and the first person I saw was Dave.

He just stared at me. Then he immediately walked over like nothing was wrong and greeted me like I was his best buddy. He gave me a huge hug. He was so happy to see me.

Over the months, he had told me all kinds of stories about the people he worked with every day and how great they all were. I had never met them, and I kind of took his stories skeptically, thinking he was maybe hyping them up a little. But the first thing he said was, "Hey, let's go meet them." I nodded, and I felt really excited for some reason.

Imagine how I was feeling. I was still starving, Lana was gone to sea for months, I hadn't slept much riding in the trucks across the continent, and I had no idea why I was really there. As I traveled, I just kept thinking about how crazy I was.

After all, I'd been trying to succeed in business for four years, and now I'd just quit my regular job and "jumped into the deep water" with both feet and no life jacket.

Then when I walked into the hotel, looking like I did, Dave just lit up and was so happy to see me. It felt really great. We walked to the elevator, got in, and headed up to meet them in their rooms.

I had just gotten there, after hitchhiking over 4,800 kilometers

> I just sobbed. Then I looked over at Dave, and he was bawling right along with me....I told myself, "These are the kinds of relationships I want."

(over 3,000 miles), and I was tired and dirty. I felt out of place, and I still wasn't sure why I'd come. But Dave wasn't mad at me for my appearance, and he didn't even care how I'd gotten there. He was that excited to see me and happy to introduce me to the leaders. It was really great. I felt so loved.

At some point in that elevator ride, all my emotions came to the surface, and I just sobbed. Then I looked over at Dave, and he was bawling right along with me, and we were both just hoping the elevator wouldn't stop so nobody would see us.

We got off on our floor, we found the right room, and we walked in to meet one of Dave's mentors. I was really intimidated to meet him because Dave had talked so much about him. But even though he had never met me before, but he looked me straight in the eyes and gave me a big smile.

He ignored the way I looked, with my combat boots and search-and-rescue clothes and a big backpack, and just walked over and gave me a big hug. He made me feel like we were already best friends. And that's when it clicked for me. I told myself, "This is it. These are the kinds of relationships I want. This is the kind of business community I want in my life."

A New Focus

After that, I was fully committed to building the right kind of community, and I just kept working harder no matter what challenges arose. The truth is it got even more difficult the next year, but I was so committed that I just kept trying to do more and do it better. As I worked, I learned six essential keys to building the right kind of relationships.

> **The truth is that everyone can succeed, but it isn't easy at all.**

Lana and my mentors helped a lot in this process, and we eventually started seeing significant success. But most people who haven't paid the price of success don't really understand what it takes. They see people with a lot of success, and they just assume they can do the same—that it won't be very difficult.

The truth is that everyone can succeed, but it isn't easy at all. It requires toughness.

It's easier, however, for those who listen to their mentors and apply the following six guidelines for great relationships. There may be even more than six, but these are the ones that made the real difference for us. Here they are:

1. Build Depth

This is the big one. A great relationship is a deep relationship. A deep relationship weathers tough times and gets us through when nothing else will. The opposite of a deep relationship is a shallow one, and a shallow relationship doesn't do anybody much good.

To create the kind of relationships that last for a lifetime, the kind you really want to last forever, build depth. Go deep.

This means spending a lot of time with those you care about most. Time builds depth, if you approach it with the right attitude. As I already mentioned, I hated that my military work kept me too busy to spend as much time as I wanted with my family.

I learned that building a great business, as much effort as it takes, actually leads to a lot more time with the family.

> "If conversation was the lyrics, laughter was the music, making time spent together a melody that could be replayed over and over without getting stale."
> —Nicholas Sparks

Of course, good communication is key to depth because as Catherine Gilbert Murdock said, "When you don't talk, there's a lot of stuff that ends up not getting said."

Emerson said it isn't the length of life but the depth of life that matters, and this applies to almost everything.

Love and Service

In relationships, depth is based on really caring about others. It is rooted in love. When I started attending a lot of big meetings after my trip to Edmonton, I heard many speakers say things like "I love you guys." I remember I used to sit in the audience and be really negative about things like that. It didn't feel authentic to me.

I couldn't understand how someone could love me without knowing me. But as we had a lot of success and I became one of the speakers in these settings, I found myself saying the same thing—and really feeling and believing it.

It was true. As I worked with more and more people, I really came to love them, their dedication and hard work, their enthusiasm and sacrifice, and their hopes and dreams for their families and their lives. I learned that it's true that we love those we serve.

When I began to make a lot of money, I also realized that our riches aren't mainly for our pleasure; they're to make it possible for us to serve more.

> As we serve, our love increases. Our bonds deepen. Our connections become stronger. And as a result, we want to serve even more.

It really does work this way. Dave served me because he saw something in me, and his success allowed him to do it. Now my success allows me to serve a lot more people than I could before. And the more I serve, the deeper my relationships grow.

Service is like the DNA of deep relationships, I think. When we stop serving, in any relationship, it dwindles. As J. K. Rowling has written, "Indifference and neglect often do much more damage than outright dislike." But the more we serve, the deeper our relationships grow.

This is especially true in marriage and family, and it is also true in business and beyond. We need to serve, and as we serve, our love increases. Our bonds deepen. Our connections become stronger. And as a result, we want to serve even more. This is a great cycle that naturally strengthens as we keep serving.

So if you ever want to improve or deepen any relationship, figure out how to truly serve the other person or people—and then get to work. Service solves so many problems. Of course, we have to serve with genuine intent to help the other people. When we do, this really works.

Sacrifice

Another part of deep relationships that is similar to love and service is sacrifice. Sadly, too many people see sacrifice as a bad thing. It seems almost everyone today wants a microwave society. They want things quick and easy, so they view sacrifice as a negative term.

They say the word *sacrifice* as if it's something bad. But my military background taught me a different way to think about sacrifice. For me, sacrifice is the production of sacred things. I sacrificed my twenties for my business, but I got the rest of my life with financial freedom.

Actually, I sacrificed leisure time, partying, going to movies twice a week, buying new cars or vacations on credit, and other things many people my age did. When I told Dave I was sacrificing these things, he said something along these lines: "The way to fail is to give up what you really want in the future for what you want immediately."

For example, I have always been a hockey fanatic. I gave up watching TV several nights a week for a few years, so now I can attend the Stanley Cup live every year. Successful leaders are those who do what others won't for a few years so that they can have what others can't for the rest of their lives.

So why do most people think of sacrifice as a bad concept, as though they're giving up something instead of creating something sacred? In the era of World War I and World War II, for example, the emotive meaning of the word *sacrifice* was good.

People lined up to join the war efforts, to sacrifice their time and even their lives for something more important. The idea of sacrificing was held in high esteem. Everyone wanted to do it.

Sacrifice meant you were going to give up something and get a lot more back. Now, too often, people think sacrifice means giving up a lot and only getting a little back. Why did this meaning change?

Over the years, I learned the answer to this question. It is usually very simple: It's because people give up *before* the sacred things happen. Most people experience a little bit of sacrifice, but they never get to the sacred things that come with sacrifice because they quit too soon.

It reminds me of the story of a grandpa who picked up his grandson for a trip. As they drove through town, the grandson started to act up a little bit, and the grandpa said, "I'll buy you an ice cream if you're good until the end of the day."

The kid yelled, "Yay!" and started being really good. After an hour, he started fidgeting a little bit. After a couple more hours, he started to play around and not listen, and the grandpa reminded him. And finally the boy asked, "How much longer?"

"Just a few more stops," the grandpa responded.

The boy said, "I can be good. But I can't be good for *this* long."

That's what I think sacrifice is like. It's about being good for long enough that you can get something sacred in your life, something wonderful you can have forever. All along the way, there are a thousand opportunities for you to quit before you get to something sacred. There are a thousand times where things will be bad enough to tempt you to give up.

> **Sacrifice is about being good for long enough that you can get something sacred in your life, something wonderful you can have forever.**

So many people have a lifestyle of cutting and running, and that's why sacrifice has become a negative idea. People want things to be easy, and that is a big lie that we tell each other—that easy is better.

I remember some parents telling me how their daughter wanted to learn to play a musical instrument. It was kind of an expensive instrument, so they waited a couple of months to make sure she was committed.

Then, finally, on the way to the store to buy the instrument, one of the parents said, "There are going to be times when you want to quit. There are going to be times when it's hard. There are going to be times when you'll go to practice instead of going out to do other things."

They were trying to prepare their daughter and create some expectations about what would bring success. Playing an instrument is a sacred skill, but you have to sacrifice some things, including time and effort, to get it.

Sacrifice is required to do great things and to build deep relationships. In addition to asking how you can serve others, ask yourself how you can sacrifice to help them. Almost nothing will make your relationship deeper than to wisely sacrifice for those you really care about.

> **Almost nothing will make your relationship deeper than to wisely sacrifice for those you really care about.**

When Lana and I first started building our business, I thought, "I'll probably be rich in a few months." But as we kept working and learning lessons for years, we built relationships with real depth. And these have made all the difference. Now, we make significant money with our business, but that stopped being what motivated us a long time ago. More than anything, we do it for the relationships.

Over the years, I learned that this is the norm. I've met with a lot of people who run big companies or have excelled in many fields and are very successful in their lives. When I started to see all the pain and sacrifice successful people from all walks of life give to their goals and purpose, I had to ask myself, "Is it still the money that motivates them?" And it's not. It might start that way, but great success is usually about truly deep relationships.

2. Use a Team Approach

The second key to really great relationships is to use the team approach. I've seen this in many ways. For example, if you want to strengthen a roof or a bridge, you make sure the foundation and supports are strong; then you add additional supports.

The same is true in relationships. Two people working in a business aren't going to get as much done as four or five—as long as everyone is committed, focused, and working hard.

And when you've got dozens of people, or even hundreds or thousands, working together toward the same vision and helping each other along the way, things feel easier, and the results are more inspiring. Teams do more than the overwhelmed lone wolf.

Sometimes people say to me, "You've got a really loyal group." It's true, and I think the reason is because so often, we work harder for some of the people on our team than they're willing to work for themselves.

We do it long enough that they start believing in themselves—and then they start doing the work. Eventually they

> "You couldn't just pick and choose at will when someone depended on you, or loved you. It wasn't like a light switch, easy to turn on or off. If you were in, you were in. Out, you were out."
> —Sarah Dessen

do it for others as much as for themselves, and when a whole group does this, the results are really amazing.

The team approach is incredibly important in marriage and family. Working together effectively is the biggest measure of a great marriage, for example. Love isn't enough if two people don't learn to master working as a team. And most people aren't born good team players; it takes some learning, practice, and humility.

The team approach is incredibly effective. As Margaret Mead put it, "Never doubt that a small group of thoughtful, committed citizens can change the world. Indeed, it is the only thing that ever has."

An essential part of working as a team, in family or business, is loyalty. Without it, things just don't work out. As military historian John Keegan wrote, "Soldiers, when committed to a task, can't compromise. It's unrelenting devotion to the standards of duty and courage, absolute loyalty to others, not letting the task go until it's been done."

Part of loyalty is putting *the team* before yourself. As you put the right priorities first, everything improves.

Sometimes people think they can have a little bit of loyalty, but you are either loyal or you're not. A good, solid 99 percent loyalty is actually 100 percent disloyalty. Would you want your spouse to be 99 percent loyal?

In addition to loyalty, unity is vital to team success. There is real power in unity. The great thinker Joseph Campbell said, "When you make the sacrifice in marriage, you're sacrificing not to each other but to unity in a relationship." And classical author Publius Syrus wrote of military operations, "Where there is unity there is always victory."

Teamwork is powerful. It's also a lot more fun than going things alone or bickering through life. We are all a lot tougher together than apart. Indeed, the quickest way to toughen up is often to build the right kind of team and really work together. Orrin Woodward reminds me often that "none of us are as good as all of us."

Buckminster Fuller and Stephen Covey both taught that in great relationships and teams, there is synergy, where the results are more than the sum of the work from everyone on the team.

To achieve real teamwork, we can't expect people to be perfect. As Donald Miller said, "When you stop expecting people to be perfect, you can like them for who they are." We have to understand that we're all just flawed and broken people doing the best we can. But if we have a shared vision that we're working toward together, we can look past the flaws by focusing on the goal.

We also have to give people the benefit of the doubt. When they do something that hurts, upsets, or frustrates us, we can't automatically assume they did it on purpose. As Henry Winkler said, "Assumptions are the termites of relationships."

People usually have good reasons for doing what they do, whether or not we understand those reasons or are upset by their actions. We have to care enough about people to listen to them and try to understand their motivations.

3. Think Long-Term

Novelist Nicholas Sparks wrote, "Every couple needs to argue now and then….Long-term relationships, the ones that matter, are all about weathering the peaks and valleys." I'm not sure about the word *need*, but I'm certain that every couple, and every close relationship for that matter, *will* have arguments.

I don't care how in sync you are with someone; there will always be misunderstandings and conflict. These start to emerge as you spend more time with a person.

You know how it goes: You meet someone for the first time. You click, and for a while, all you see are the good things about them. But then you spend more time with them, and stuff they do starts bugging you.

Maybe you don't like how they chew, or you get sick of them telling the same story over and over again. Maybe they say something that really touches a deep wound in you, and you get offended.

You have to learn to push through all that junk by making the relationship more important than your feelings and your pain. And you have to be willing to have the hard conversations and communicate with each other when you've been hurt.

Harboring resentments kills relationships over the long term. By being honest in relationships, with conversations that may seem tough in the moment, we can break through barriers and get even closer. But if we just stew over stuff without communicating, or cut and run every time we experience conflict, the relationship can never excel.

I think a lot of times we're afraid to be honest about stuff that bugs us because we're afraid of damaging the relationship. But if we do it in a respectful way, that honesty actually builds trust. Far too many people will never have those tough conversations with the person they're upset with, but they'll rag on them to other people behind their backs.

That erodes trust. To quote Nicholas Sparks again, "Every couple has ups and downs, every couple argues, and that's the thing—you're a couple, and couples can't function without trust." Again, that holds true for any relationship, not just with our spouses.

The story is told of a couple whose family threw a party for their fiftieth wedding anniversary. The whole family and a lot of friends attended. There was dancing, food, and a huge celebration at a local hotel. At the end of the evening of partying, they released fifty helium balloons—one for each of the years they had been married—to float to the ballroom's high ceiling.

The next morning, family members went to clean up the room where the party had been held. Some of the balloons were still up at the ceiling, some had drifted to the floor, and still others floated at different levels in the air.

The father who had been married for fifty years pointed out that marriage is like those balloons. "Some years are up, some years are down, and some are in between. But none of them have popped," he said. "That's the important thing."

That's how great relationships are, and the down years help make the up years even better.

4. Take Initiative; Your Leaders Will Follow You

Another key to relationships is to take initiative. Yes, your colleagues and other leaders are there to help you. But that doesn't mean you should sit around waiting for them to tell you what to do.

Don't leave the responsibility of the relationship and your success up to your leaders. Take initiative in building relationships with them. You'll be amazed by how much time and attention they'll invest in you if you take initiative. The passion of the protégé determines the impartation of the mentor.

And I'm not just talking about picking their brains and being a leech. I'm talking about doing the hard work. When you take initiative, other leaders take notice—and action.

When Lana and I started our business, we lived in a tiny apartment with white cupboards in the kitchen located at 64 Lakefront Road. We made more mistakes than I can count. We were so clueless. We were just desperate to find a way to make it work. We weren't capable, but we were really willing. So we spent a lot of time looking for competent people to help us.

We wrote our goals for our first week on those white kitchen cupboards, with what we thought was a dry-erase marker. (For all we know, those goals are still on those cupboards.) We thought we were going to get rich that week. Do you know we lived in that apartment for four years, and we never reached those goals we had set for our first week?

That's not something we're ashamed of. A lot of people carry around goals they set a long time ago. But instead of remembering that there was a time when they believed in them, they keep them as proof that they have failed.

I congratulate them for even having the courage to set a goal because most people spend their life never knowing what it's like to really believe in something.

One time, Dave came over to our house. Lana was washing dishes in the kitchen, and I was taking a nap while Dave was on the phone. Lana remembers that she was having kind of a pity party because we had been in the business three years, and we still weren't doing great. Then she overheard part of Dave's phone conversation. She tried not to eavesdrop. But it was a small apartment, so it was hard not to hear.

What she heard him say changed our lives forever. "Ah, really," he said. "That's so amazing. Are you okay? Was Mom there? Did she get it on film?" Lana started realizing that something big must have happened with Dave's family back home while he was sitting in our living room.

He continued, "Jason, I'm so proud of you, and I'm so sorry I missed your valedictorian speech today."

Lana said she felt like crawling into a hole.

"Claude and Lana needed me more, and I told them I would come," he continued. "I knew you'd understand."

Lana felt like a knife had been shoved through her heart. The sad thing is, after three years, that was the first time we understood the sacrifice this man was making for us. Up until that point, it didn't cost us anything. We knew he'd come out, month after month, to help us, and I suppose we had taken that for granted a little.

He had given us such a critical day in his life. And what had we done to deserve that?

It has been many years since Dave's son crossed the stage as valedictorian. Lana and I have tried, every single moment of our lives every single day since then, to make good on that trade. We owe him that.

> There are people who are making sacrifices for you....How hard are you willing to fight to honor those sacrifices?

There are people who are making sacrifices for you. There are people who are selling memories to you. What have you done to make good on those trades? When you deserve those trades, will you be proud of

what you have done to deserve them? How hard are you willing to fight to honor those sacrifices?

It was because of Dave's sacrifice that I was willing to hitch-
hike across Canada to get to that event in Edmonton. And
like I said, you'll be amazed by how much your leaders will be
willing to sacrifice and invest in you if you take initiative too.

5. Master the Basics

Another key of relationships is to master the basics. The
little things are so important. For example, I love Hawaii. I especially enjoy surfing. I'm not the best at it, but I go out there
and watch the people who have been surfing a specific break
since they were four or five years old.

Over many years, they've mastered the basics of that spot in
the ocean. They know it well, and I like to see how they surf it
differently than those of us who don't have their experience. I
know that their wisdom is at a whole different level than mine.

Once I was out there looking for a wave, and all the "out-
siders" like me were just watching the ocean hoping a wave
would come. But suddenly all the surfers who had been surfing
in this spot for ten or fifteen years were paddling.

I wondered what was happening. I couldn't see anything.
But they were paddling, and I knew the power of experience.
So I just turned and started paddling like crazy.

I learned that the most important time to start paddling, at
least when you're dealing with the big waves, is when the wave
is right under you—before you see it as a wave. Because when it
finally swells up above the surface and rises high into the air, it's
too late to start paddling. Thankfully, by watching those with
experience, I was able to catch some of the best waves.

It's the same in relationships. If we master the basics and
apply them day after day, we'll be in the right place doing the
right thing when some big wave comes along—either a prob-

lem or an opportunity. If we aren't doing the basics, we won't be prepared, and our relationships will suffer or even crack under the pressure.

And just as with surfing, the way to know what to do is to watch those who are really successful. That's why I give so much honor to my mentors and why I'll travel far and pay a lot just to spend a few minutes with them. I know I can watch how they handle things, and in so doing, I learn the basics and how to master them.

So when my mentors start paddling in some direction, I match their energy, passion, and pace. Then when the wave breaks, I'm hanging out with the veterans instead of stuck back on a still ocean with all the rookies.

If you want to lead, if you want to live up to your best potential, you've got to keep your eye on good mentors and master the basics. In fact, part of mastering the basics is being an effective follower of the right mentors and principles.

Two books that really helped us learn this lesson are *The 5 Love Languages* and *Personality Plus*. I highly recommend both of these great studies on relationships.

6. Use Big Events to Reach the Heart

In all of this, seminars and other events can be your secret weapon, just like church meetings or AA meetings. There's nothing like a big meeting with good speakers and a lot of energy to really help business owners catch the vision of what a community is all about.

In the end, it's about relationships: improving relationships with your family by gaining more freedom and developing better, more meaningful friendships with leaders who share your values and vision.

Seminars help us see the kind of people we'll be associating with when we build a business. They attract like-minded people who are driven to be better and do more, people who really want to make a difference in the world.

I'm a huge believer in the power of association, and seminars and events have been vital to our business growth. One time, there was a winter event I wanted to get to, but I didn't have the money to make the trip.

So I went out and got a job as a security guard. I had just gotten out of the military, so basically, I went from protecting the prime minister to protecting a liquor store. I remember standing there in the cold realizing how much things had changed.

The day of Christmas Eve, I guarded that liquor store from 10:00 a.m. to 4:00 p.m. After that, I went to the mall and did a twelve-hour security shift from 7:00 p.m. to 7:00 a.m. Then I went home and spent time with Lana for a couple of hours, and then I went and did a few more shifts.

It was very humbling. I had just worked security at the G7, and now I was in a small backward town at the edge of nowhere. I went from protecting dignitaries to being a mall cop. In fact, none of the real mall cops wanted to work on Christmas, so they brought in a low-grade mall cop: *me*. Talk about humbling.

Over the week of Christmas, I put in a ton of hours and made a couple of grand because I was getting paid double time and a half. And because of that, I was able to go to the function. I remember how humbling this was, as I said already, *and* how this experience got me to start thinking long-term.

If you can get people to seminars and events, you'll have a much higher chance of really connecting with them—whatever your business and whatever you care about. They'll feel the energy. They'll see the sincerity of real leaders. They'll want to develop long-term relationships with you and other people like you.

Carl Jung said, "The meeting of two personalities is like the contact of two chemical substances: if there is any reaction, both are transformed." Getting someone to a good event makes that "chemical reaction" even more potent.

Relationships Are Power

Over time, I have become more and more convinced that our business is vitally important. It can make a difference in many relationships. We don't need to invite greatness; we need to truly promote it. By doing this, we will have people who care about the world and champion a cause.

When we have a lot of people working and fighting for something, we can make a huge difference. We need to be the people who will attract others with our truth. We need to live what we believe. That is the cause of leadership, and that is our responsibility to our cause.

Living for a great cause will probably be the most challenging journey you've ever been on. It will take you to places you don't always want to go. But when you look back, you'll realize it was the best journey you've ever taken.

It will make you aware of how incredibly important you are to people. You can touch and change many lives when you decide to live a life of greatness and significance, when you decide to commit your life to helping people feel alive.

> You can touch and change many lives when you decide to live a life of greatness and significance, when you decide to commit your life to helping people feel alive.

Lana and I were only contacted once with the business opportunity we ended up building. That's right: just *one* time. One person thought to say, "Hey, I have this thing you might be interested in."

Can you imagine if that person had quit before getting to us? I think about that all the time. It haunts me because if that person had given up, we would probably still be in the navy. Lana would probably be floating around in the Atlantic somewhere, three shades of green from seasickness. And our family? I don't even want to think about that.

But we're where we are today because of one relationship that made all the difference. Who will *you* make the difference for, and what will their lives be like because you cared about them and showed them a better way?

PART THREE

The Pointy Tip

The spines of the weak stiffen in the
presence of the bold.

Man is only great when he acts from passion.
—Benjamin Disraeli

STRENGTH SEVEN
PASSION

"Passion amplifies effort."

I want to say right at the start of this chapter that passion, real passion, changes everything. Look at your life, your marriage, and your career. Are you passionate about these things or just lukewarm? Are you trying with all your heart to get into heaven, or are you just hoping not to end up in hell? Are you striving and working your best to have a truly great marriage? Or are you just trying to avoid getting divorced? Are you trying to get truly financially fit, even wealthy, or are you just working to not get fired? Passion makes all the difference!

Passion is what convinced me to get into business for myself in the first place. As I mentioned earlier, I didn't have a lot of success at first. But I wanted something better for Lana. Sometimes people tell me they think that building a business is easy for me because I don't know what it's like to be broke.

Are you kidding me? We were broke for years. We were so broke that we drove an old $400 car that could have fallen apart at any moment. There was a small hole in the gas tank, so when we put gas in, we'd go around smelling like fuel for the rest of the day.

I have been so broke that I cried, wondering how I would ever turn things around. I've felt devastated when an exciting new prospect called me back and told me he wasn't interested because his brother-in-law would "beat him up" for joining me in business.

More times than I can count, I have given a speech late at night and been too amped up to sleep well and then flown to a new place and repeated the process day after day. After a few days, I would drag myself into the next meeting looking like a gang had attacked me in the parking lot. I could go on and on.

In all this, though, I felt real passion when I imagined how we could have a better life. Passion kept me going. And when the success came and we weren't broke anymore, I felt even more passion for my work. When we became financially independent and I knew my wife and kids would always have what they needed, my passion grew even more.

One time, a local newspaper interviewed us and did a two-page spread about our beautiful old house after we'd been in it for just a year. Lana and I didn't feel we had changed all that much until we started answering the reporter's questions.

When we read the article, it dawned on us that it was the same newspaper that we had previously used to look for jobs. We used to pore over the classified ads looking for ways to make an extra fifty bucks to pay our Visa bill or fill up our gas tank that month.

So I look at things now, a few years down the road, and think how different our circumstances have become because of our passion and commitment. It's incredible to me. Having a life is more than making a living. But we have to *earn* it. We have to put on our suit of armor and say, "I'm not going down without a fight. This ain't over till I say it's over."

Our flames of passion must be stronger than the downpour of challenges.

Know this: Your tomorrow is more exciting than your today. It can be tough to push through those low points when you've worked so hard and so long and it feels like you're not making the least bit of progress.

It's during those times that it's most important to dig deep and tap into your passion. It is worth every fight that you could possibly drum up inside you. You will be so proud of yourself when you meet the person you are capable of being. Our flames of passion must be stronger than the downpour of challenges.

Passion Makes Up for Lack of Skill

Passion, like hard work, can overcome a lack of skill. You may not be the best presenter. You may not have the best people skills. You may not have all the answers. You may feel weak and inadequate to your task.

But when you act and speak from passion, it is electrifying and contagious. People will be drawn to you. Sure, you'll turn some people off too, but they're the ones who probably would have been turned off no matter what you did. And even the ones who are turned off will eventually come to respect your commitment if you stick with it.

When you start out as a leader or building a business, you'll be lacking in knowledge and skill. But passion can make up for those deficiencies. It's what will push you through the tough experiences. It's the catalyst for learning.

It also helps you conquer fear. Passion makes us believe in ourselves when no one or nothing else does and it seems like the world is against us.

I was once asked to participate in a panel discussion. A gentleman interviewed us, and we began discussing lack of faith. He asked all the panelists, "Have you ever doubted that you'd be successful in business?"

The question went around to all the other panelists, and they gave what seemed to me like politically correct answers, basically admitting that yes, they had doubted themselves.

When it came around to me and the interviewer asked me the question, I said, point blank, "No." It wasn't because I was arrogant. It was simply because I truly believed in myself. I had an unquenchable fire of passion burning in my belly.

Come heck or high water, I was going to be financially independent. I was going to change the world. I was going to lead people to achieve their greatness. That's all there was to it. End of story.

I had been told many times that nobody in my region of Canada had ever reached the highest level of my business, but I just felt that if I kept trying, I'd eventually make it. Passion works.

Joss Whedon wrote:

> Passion. It lies in all of us. Sleeping…waiting…and though unwanted, unbidden, it will stir, open its jaws and howl. It speaks to us, guides us. Passion rules us all. And we obey. What other choice do we have? Passion is the source of our finest moments.
>
> The joy of love, the clarity of hatred, the ecstasy of grief. It hurts sometimes more than we can bear. If we could live without passion, maybe we'd know some kind of peace. But we would be hollow. Empty rooms, shuttered and dank. Without passion, we'd be truly dead.

That's how I've always felt: What other choice did I have but to obey the passion within me? And slowly but surely, as I acted on my passion, it transformed into knowledge and skill.

Orrin Woodward and Oliver DeMille talk about "credentialists" in their book *LeaderShift*. These are people who put a lot of stock in degrees, credentials, résumés, and worldly credibility. They look down their noses at guys like me who may not have a wall full of degrees in fancy frames but who are bursting with passion.

The thing is most credentialists will never change the world—in fact, their goal is usually to preserve the status quo for their benefit. They'll never be a real force for freedom or innovation. They're too busy trying to look good to the world. They're more concerned with appearing smart than doing good.

It's the passionate ones, ruffians and rascals though we may be, who really make a difference. As Jim Butcher wrote, "Passion has overthrown tyrants and freed prisoners and slaves. Passion has brought justice where there was savagery. Passion has created freedom where there was nothing but fear. Passion has helped souls rise from the ashes of their horrible lives and build something better, stronger, more beautiful."

Most credentialists will never make as great a difference in the world as passionate, rough-around-the-edges, mission-driven people.

Now, I'm not knocking sincere scholarship. Learning is definitely a critical component of success and something I'm always striving to do. I'm simply making the point that book knowledge isn't required to get started and to make a difference. If all you have is passion, that's enough

> **If all you have is passion, that's enough to get started. But if you have knowledge with no passion, then you're unlikely to succeed.**

to get started. But if you have knowledge with no passion, then you're unlikely to succeed.

Likewise, if you care more about what people say about you than what you do for other people, I think that's sad. As Nicholas Sparks said, "The saddest people I've ever met in life are the ones who don't care deeply about anything at all. Passion and satisfaction go hand in hand, and without them, any happiness is only temporary, because there's nothing to make it last."[64]

I like how the great classical historian Thucydides put it: "The nation that makes a great distinction between its scholars and its warriors will have its thinking done by cowards and its fighting done by fools."

"Sacred Suffering"

When we dig into the roots of the word *passion*, we discover some enlightening truths. Look it up in the dictionary, and you'll find the following definitions:

- Strong and barely controllable emotion
- A state or outburst of such emotion
- Intense romantic love
- An intense desire or enthusiasm for something
- A thing arousing enthusiasm

But in our culture of shortcuts and convenience, we've lost the depth and true meaning of passion. The word was coined by twelfth-century religious scholars, who created it to describe the "willing suffering of Christ."

Kevin Hall describes how he learned about the roots of this word from a retired Stanford linguistics professor named Arthur:

> After educating me about the word's [origin], Arthur added, "Passion doesn't mean just suffering for suffering's sake; it must be pure and willing suffering." Arthur said that both "passion" and "path" have similar roots: the word "path" is a suffix that means *suffering from*.
>
> "Think about it, Kevin," said Arthur. "We have doctors called pathologists. They study the illnesses and diseases that humans suffer."
>
> Then he revealed a link between suffering, or passion, and sacrifice. "The word *sacrifice* comes from the Latin *sacra*, which means *sacred*, and *fice*, which means to *perform*. To sacrifice is to *perform the sacred*."
>
> "At its essence," he continued, "passion is sacred suffering."

Kevin concludes that:

It's one thing to suffer and be a victim; it's an entirely different thing to be willing to suffer for a cause and become a victor. Even though it has become popular to define passion as deep or romantic love, the real meaning is *being willing to suffer for what you love*. **When we discover what we are willing to pay a price for, we discover our life's mission and purpose**.

> "It's one thing to suffer and be a victim; it's an entirely different thing to be willing to suffer for a cause and become a victor."
> —Kevin Hall

Wow. That's toughness. Think about it: Passion isn't just what excites us. It's what we're willing to suffer and sacrifice for. This puts the word in a whole new light, doesn't it? This is especially deep with its connection to the suffering of Christ.

His passion wasn't some superficial emotion that made Him excited. It was a deep commitment to a profound cause, which gave Him the strength to carry His own cross and then die on it.

"Passion," said Mark Z. Danielewski, "has little to do with euphoria and everything to do with patience. It is not about feeling good. It is about endurance. Like patience, passion comes from the same Latin root: *pati*. It does not mean to flow with exuberance. It means to suffer." We only really have something worth living for when we are willing to sacrifice.

Are you engaged in a cause you're willing to suffer and even die for? Or are you just trying to make money so you can drive a fancy car and lounge on the beach? I suppose that's your prerogative, and you have the freedom to live your life any way you see fit.

But the thing about liberty and family and leadership, which we so often take for granted, is that they're sacred. Freedom was given to us by people who suffered, bled, and died. It took a lot of people bound together and doing the right thing for a long time to earn our freedom.

And now our countries are full of too many people who are unwilling to sacrifice anything to gain something sacred.

Hacky Sack Lessons

You know what it reminds me of? All the people who camped out and occupied Wall Street a while back. Now you've got to be upset to camp out on Wall Street in October. That's passion, all right.

These people were mad about something, and their passion spread. But most of them weren't even mad about the same thing. The police couldn't go in and arrest the ringleaders because nobody seemed to know who they even were.

They did a protest like that in Halifax, and somebody forgot to bring the megaphone, so it was a really silent protest. A bunch of people stood around on the corners playing hacky sack.

Most of them didn't even know exactly what they were mad about, but they wanted to do something, change something. They didn't know what they wanted to change exactly, and they weren't sure *how* to change things.

I think we can learn from the passion of people who are willing to protest for something they care about. But I don't want to be just a protester; I want to be a doer. I want to be a sacrificer. I want to create something sacred. I want to leave a legacy. I want to add value to the lives of others. And that doesn't come easy. A price must be paid; sacrifices must be made to do something meaningful in life. As Albert Camus said, "There is scarcely any passion without struggle."

The Pursuit of Excellence

Life isn't just about winning; it's about excellence. It's not just about getting what we want; it's about doing everything we undertake with excellence, whether anyone notices or whether we get paid to do it.

It's about constantly striving to become better today than we were yesterday, to achieve our full potential. Passion pushes us to excellence.

That's why I have loved building our business. It has inspired us to try to pursue excellence in every aspect of our lives. I mean, a guy can be super successful in business and make a ton of money, but is he really living a life of excellence if his family is in shambles? If his relationship with God is being neglected? If he's not serving his community? If his health is failing?

Money can be overrated. I knew a guy who once inherited $4.3 million. But it took him less than three years to squander it all away. He was a big guy, and he came to my house one time riding a $5,000 bike. "Wow! What an amazing bike!" I said.

He responded, "Yeah, I'm going to lose some weight. I figured if I bought this it would make me lose weight." You know what? He rode it two times. Then, when he was going broke, I bought that $5,000 bike from him for $500.

The fact that he had money didn't change the fact that he had bad habits. As Aristotle and Will Durant put it, "We are what we repeatedly do. Excellence, then, is not an act, but a habit." This guy wasn't living the excellence ethic. Having a lot of money turned him apathetic. He figured he didn't have to keep working hard to improve himself.

You hear lots of stories like this about people who win the lottery or otherwise inherit a bunch of money without having worked to earn it. The lessons of success are very important, and it takes time and struggle to learn them well.

When Lana and I turned the corner in our business, it turned fast. Financially, life became easier. But we didn't want to rest on our laurels. So we set higher goals, and then we announced them to the world.

Whenever you announce your goals, your adversary is revealed. We wanted more than just money. We wanted to find a cause and belong to a home and a team. As soon as we announced those goals and made those intentions, our adversaries were revealed.

Life can be hard. That's why we need to be tough.

> **When you strive for excellence, you're not content with having everything you want and living the life of your dreams. You want to do everything in your power to serve and uplift others and inspire them to excellence.**

We had the material things, but we wanted more significant things. We chose to take the hard way out *now*, on purpose, knowing that our lives *would* get easier, and because of that, we would be able to make others' lives better.

We also wanted to mentor other people to get to our level. That's part of the excellence ethic—teaching it to others so that they, too, can enjoy its fruits. When you strive for excellence, you're not content with having everything you want and living the life of your dreams. You want to do everything in your power to serve and uplift others and inspire them to excellence.

Achieving excellence means you have to sacrifice what you want now for what you want most of all. As the famous dancer Mikhail Baryshnikov noted, "To achieve some depth in your field requires a lot of sacrifices." Lana and I had to give up a lot of evening and weekend hours. We had to sacrifice mental and emotional comfort. We had to surrender who we were in order to become who we wanted to be.

This is a huge part of real toughness—being willing to say no to the unimportant things, even when it would be easy to say yes, in order to really fight for the important stuff. Passion means finding something you're willing to be tough about and then *living* that toughness.

Vision: The Passion Generator

When we're obsessively focused on a goal we're truly passionate about, we'll stop at nothing to get it. But here's the thing: passion can be lost. It's not some inexhaustible resource in our souls completely independent of our thinking. It's generated by our thoughts and our choices.

If we get overwhelmed by challenges, it can be easy to sink into negative thinking. And when we do, it's easy to lose sight of our passion. Sometimes it's just too easy to justify quitting.

We have to learn how to be our own passion generators in our darkest moments. This is done by having a clear and compelling vision of who we want to be and what we want to have and achieve. We have to know exactly what we want. We have to be able to see it, feel it, taste it, hear it, and smell it. And we have

> We have to learn how to be our own passion generators in our darkest moments.

to hold fast to that vision no matter what, especially when it seems like we'll never achieve it.

Acting on passion to achieve a vision is a form of faith. It takes faith to make phone calls, set up appointments, show up to presentations night after night—or whatever you do in your line of work. But if your cause is just and your passion is strong enough, your faith *will* be rewarded.

Your job is to keep your faith, keep your vision in front of you, and do the work for a long enough time that success comes.

After years of hard and seemingly fruitless work, our energy can be drained, our passion lost, our vision faded. That's when we need passion the most. And that's when we need to learn how to generate it ourselves because no one else can do it for us. We can go to motivational seminars, we can read books, and we can talk to mentors. But ultimately, our drive has to come from within.

What is your vision of your ideal life? What kind of person are you? What do you have inside that you want to become? How do you spend your time? What does it feel like to be living that life? Have you written all this down? Do you keep it in front of you at all times? Is your vision big and compelling enough to be stronger than your pain and fear? Is it clear enough to outweigh your challenges?

Passion gives you strength and energy to overcome obstacles. But you have to generate it yourself. And when you learn to do that consistently over time, there will come a time when you've accomplished your goals and you get to plan even bigger ones.

> **Passion makes us tough because when it is bigger than our struggles, bigger than our challenges, bigger than our shortcomings, it can pull us through when everything else seems to fail.**

That's what passion does. Passion makes us tough because when it is bigger than our struggles, bigger than our challenges, bigger than our shortcomings, it can pull us through when everything else seems to fail.

If you keep living in this kind of passion, you'll keep going no matter what. And eventually, you'll look back at your life and be amazed at how far you've come because of your passion and commitment.

But the best thing about a life of passion is this: for every goal you meet, you'll just increase your passion for the next one. Imagine how powerful this can be in our life. And how much positive impact and influence it will have on other people you care about.

Passion changes everything because it takes things to the next level.

*Let me tell you the secret that has led me to my goal. My
strength lies solely in my tenacity.*
—Louis Pasteur

STRENGTH EIGHT

TENACITY

"Quitters quit everything."

Imagine that you're riding a white horse. To your side, a lion is
glaring at you menacingly. On the other side, a group of zebras is
running wild. In front of you, gazelles and a giraffe are jumping
and running. Behind you, a stampede of horses is bearing down
on you.

Clearly, you're in a tough spot. So what are you going to do to
get out of this mess? The answer is
easy: get your drunken self off the
merry-go-round!

Not every challenge in life is so
easy to overcome. Sometimes we
have to really fight to get out of our
messes and create the life we want.
And sometimes it's not so much a
matter of proactively fighting as it is just holding on until the storm
passes.

> "Success seems to
> be largely a matter
> of hanging on after
> others let go."
> —William Feather

In fact, the word *tenacity* comes from the Latin *tenacitas*, which
means "the act of holding fast."

That reminds me of a cartoon depicting a bird trying to swal-
low a frog. The frog is reaching out of the bird's mouth and hold-

ing on to the bird's neck for all he's worth, and the caption reads, "NEVER, NEVER, NEVER, NEVER GIVE UP!"

Keep Going!

I've seen many people quit when they were so close to success. In his classic *Think and Grow Rich*, Napoleon Hill shares a poignant story illustrating why this is so foolish. Seized by "gold fever" in the Gold Rush days, a man went west to dig for wealth. He staked a claim and started digging with a pick and shovel. After weeks of labor, he was rewarded with the shine of ore. But he needed machinery to bring it to the surface.

So he covered up his mine and went to borrow money from family and friends. They bought the machinery, and he went to work on the mine. The first car of ore was mined and shipped to a smelter. From all appearances, they had struck one of the richest mines in Colorado. After a few more cars of ore, they would clear their debts and make a killing in profits.

But as they continued drilling, the vein of gold ore disappeared. They had reached the end of the rainbow and found no pot of gold. They kept drilling in desperation, but the vein eluded them. So they quit, sold the machinery to a junk man for a few hundred dollars, and took the train back home in defeat.

The junk man to whom they had sold the equipment called in a mining engineer. They did some calculations. The engineer said the project had failed because the owners didn't know about "fault lines."

He calculated that the vein would be found just three feet from where they had stopped drilling. And that was exactly where it was found. The junk man made millions of dollars from the mine.

"Many of life's failures," said Thomas Edison, "are people who did not realize how close they were to success when they gave up."[65] Amen, Thomas, amen.

The closer you are to your goal, the less timid you can afford to be. And since it's often difficult to see how close we are to real achievement, we should just get in the habit of being more and more passionate as we go along.

I love a cartoon that expresses this idea really well. In fact, it runs along the same lines as Hill's gold mine story.

On one side of the picture, there's a huge cache of diamonds. On the other end, there are two men with mining tools. One of the men is still quite a distance from the diamonds, but you can see his passion and tenacity in the way he runs toward them with his pickaxe.

The other man is less than a foot from the diamonds; only a tiny bit of dirt separates him from success. Unfortunately, this man has just turned around, head hung and shoulders slumped, to go home.

The caption on this cartoon also reads: "NEVER GIVE UP!"

Sometimes you can't tell how far away the cache of diamonds is, but if you are constantly feeding your passion and your drive, you can be the guy who actually increases his forward momentum as he goes.

NEVER GIVE UP!

Expect Hard

We give up when we expect life to be easy. A few years back, my brother, who was twenty-three at the time, and his wife were coming out to visit us for the holidays. I paid for their plane tickets. I wasn't supposed to, but I talked to them in July and asked if they had them yet. They said no, so I decided I would just buy the tickets to save them the extra money they would have to pay if they waited until the last minute.

He called me a couple months after I'd bought the plane tickets and told me about an "awesome" TV he had just purchased. He raved on and on about all the cool things it did. Then he said, "I got it for $800."

I said, "Wait a second. You just spent $800 on a TV after I bought your plane tickets?"

He responded, "Well, I didn't have to give them any money."

"So how'd you get it, then?" I asked. "Did you steal it?"

"No, I just had to get the store credit card."

"Ah," I said. "But you know you'll end up paying a lot more than $800 then, right?"

We did the math and figured out he'd eventually pay $2,300 for that TV. I know that if he were to walk down the aisle of a store and see that same TV for $2,300, he'd say, "Who's the moron who'd pay that much for that TV?"

Those are the kinds of decisions we make when we want things fast and easy. But life—true life, life worth living—doesn't come fast and easy. It takes hard work and sacrifice. It takes tenacity.

Funny thing is, it required a certain kind of tenacity for my brother to pay that stupid TV off—because he forced himself to make the payments. But why not display a little emotional toughness and willingness to sacrifice up front, thereby saving a lot of money and effort down the road?

Here's the thing: You don't pay a price to chase your dreams; you pay a price if you *don't* chase your dreams. Trials and hard times come to everyone. It's not a matter of *if* you'll have difficulties; it's a matter of *when*. Life is pretty much tough on each of us, whether we decide to lie down and take it or choose to be tough right back.

Tenacity means you know that tough times are coming sooner or later, and instead of wondering about the ifs and whens, you get ready to face them by asking about the *how*s. How will you prepare yourself to meet challenges, how will you react when they come, and how will you overcome them?

Some people live in a dream world, and some live in reality. There is also a third group, who turn one into the other. These are the people who know that difficulties will come but choose to make their success outweigh the challenges.

These are the ones who say, "It's not a matter of *if* I will achieve my dreams and find real success; it's a matter of *when*." And then they figure out how they're going to make it happen, and they never stop

> You don't pay a price to chase your dreams; you pay a price if you *don't* chase your dreams.

fighting for their dream reality. They become less timid—and more committed—with every step they take.

It's So Worth It

I remember another young couple who were family friends, so I flew out several times to help them when they were starting their own business. At first, they were pretty sure they were going to be rich in a few months, which I understood because that was exactly how I felt when I started.

After about a year, they started moaning, and they said, "We're broke, and we fight all the time, and we're tired." They made a long list of reasons why their life was terrible. They were making four or five hundred dollars a month from their business, and they were using it to invest back into building their company.

After they told me a bunch of their problems and concerns, I finally said, "I can fix this tonight. We'll meet, and I'll fix it all."

They were enthused, and we met for dinner. I said, "Tell me specifically what's wrong."

The ironic thing was that they had about the fewest responsibilities adults can have. They had no children or pets, not even a goldfish. They didn't have demanding jobs, just themselves to look after.

After they finished telling me the problems, I nodded. Then I started talking: "Well, I can fix this right away. I can get some money in your pocket tomorrow! Cancel your business meetings tonight."

They had plans to drive an hour for a couple of sales meetings, and I said, "Do not go on those meetings. Don't lose that money on gas. You won't use your sales samples, and I need some so I'll buy them from you. Instant cash."

They were looking at me in amazement, so I kept going. "The next thing is sell your tickets to the big training meeting that is coming up. Get rid of them; save that Saturday to stay at home and watch TV.

"I know you don't have cable right now because you cut it, but you can get cable, and you'll probably stop fighting. You'll basically sit there and be brainwashed by whatever's on every night.

"You'll laugh at the same time, cry at the same time, get mad at the same time—you'll be like in-sync robots. No more fighting; it'll be perfect."

By this point, they had figured out what I was doing, but I didn't stop. "I can make your life easy by taking away your hardships. I'll take away every single thing you're doing to produce something down the road.

"You can focus on trying to live in the Instant Society. And if you run into any problems, just call me, and I'll tell you more ways to take the easy path and do nothing that will require hard work or difficulty.

"But in the process, you'll create nothing sacred. I can let you stay in your circumstances, or I can offer you your dreams."

I could see that they were really feeling it, so I added, "If you argue for your limitations hard enough, you'll get to keep them."

The Trap of Now

I think that's one of the problems we have right now. We used to have a lot of sacred things, including family, liberty, and free enterprise. These sacred things didn't come instantaneously. And neither will financial freedom or leadership in your personal life.

For some reason, there are so many people who want instant success, and they think something is wrong if they have to work for it. So

> There are so many people who want instant success... So often, they're not willing to sacrifice anything to get to something sacred.

often, they're not willing to sacrifice anything to get to something sacred.

But for those who are willing, it is oh, so worth it. Life becomes much easier and more fulfilling after you've pushed through the hard stuff.

Lana has this weird addiction where she gets sucked into movies on airplanes. She watched *Marley and Me* something like eighteen times. Even though she cries every time, she keeps watching it.

Anyway, she tells the story about watching a movie about a young girl who's a surfing champion at the height of her success. Everything seems to be going right when a huge change happens, and she has to decide whether she's going to let this change defeat her or make it define her.

Lana will admit that before we started building our business, she was one of those people who let crises defeat her because she felt powerless to change and affect her future. But the more we grew in our business, she realized that crises don't have to defeat us. Instead, they can define us because it's in the trenches that we discover who we truly are and what we're truly capable of.

So this young girl is going through this toil. She goes to church one day, still stuck in the mind-set of, "Why did this have to happen? Why me?" Her youth pastor shows her an image on a screen and says, "What do you think this is?" The image has been magnified, so it looks like a sponge or a dishcloth. But when the pastor zooms out, it is actually the eye of a fly.

This was a big lesson for Lana. As she explains it, we look at our crises and challenges through distorted lenses. What we see through those lenses determines how we choose and act. But often it's not the problem that's the problem—it's how we *view* the problem. If we just choose to focus on the positive and continue working and holding on, eventually we'll start seeing with new eyes. We'll see what we can't see right now.

This young surfer was focused on the challenges. But she needed to understand that she lacked perspective on how to fix those challenges. She needed to have faith, to understand that somebody had a plan for her.

We all need to keep our perspectives open enough, and hang on long enough, to get to the end of the plan. It is so worth it. Faith is always going to make you wait; it's always going to make you ache, but it will always be rewarded. Faith is vitally important. It's required in every part of life.

> **We don't always get what we deserve, and we don't get what we want sometimes, but we will always get what we expect.**

We don't always get what we deserve, and we don't get what we want sometimes, but we will always get what we expect. It's not going to be easy. When that young girl had to relearn everything, it wasn't easy. But the thing that she thought was going to leave her on her knees ended up defining her. Her reserves of faith, strength, and determination and her potential skills would have stayed simmering below the surface if that crisis had not come.

Be glad for the bumps and the scrapes. Be glad for the challenges and the days of lack of faith. And be glad for the journey because the journey is ultimately the prize. It's what defines you. And who you become is worth the journey.

As Amelia Earhart said, "The most difficult thing is the decision to act; the rest is merely tenacity. The fears are paper tigers. You can do anything you decide to do. You can act to change and control your life; and the procedure, the process, is its own reward."[66]

Make It a Movement

I want to tell any people who want to quit to toughen up—to get a life and figure out what is really important to them and fight for it. And I mean that in the spirit of love.

The truth is building a family and a successful business is a movement. It's a cause. It's never perfect, but it's worth fighting for. It's worth taking action to build. Or if your life purpose is something else, then that is worth fighting for. But without taking a stand, without realizing that life isn't supposed to be easy—what's it all for?

Life is tough. Life is risky. Living up to our potential takes hard, persistent work. And that's exactly why it pays such high dividends. We get what we pay for at the store, and life is no different. We get what we're willing to pay for. If all we're willing to pay for is petty comfort and fearful security, then we'll get it. But that comes at the cost of what we could have become.

Helen Keller said, "Life is either a daring adventure or nothing. Security does not exist in nature, nor do the children of men as a whole experience it. Avoiding danger is no safer in the long run than exposure." That's the funny thing: Striving for comfort and security is every bit as risky as striving for greatness. Yet somehow people think that taking a stand, standing out, trying to become better, and starting a business are the risky things.

> **When you make your life about a cause and a movement bigger than your own selfish concerns, you're much more likely to push through the hard times.**

When you make your life about a cause and a movement bigger than your own selfish concerns, you're much more likely to push through the hard times. Viktor Frankl, the great psychiatrist, Nazi concentration camp survivor, and author of *Man's Search for Meaning*, counseled:

Don't aim at success. The more you aim at it and make it a target, the more you are going to miss it.

For success, like happiness, cannot be pursued; it must ensue, and it only does so as the unintended side effect of one's personal dedication to a cause greater than oneself or as the by-product of one's surrender to a person other than oneself.

You'll find that trying to make money just so you can live a comfortable life will never be motivation enough. That motivation is as weak as the desire is petty. This is about changing the world. This is about leaving things better than we found them. This is about fighting for freedom and free enterprise and families. This is about giving our family opportunities. It's not about us.

Lana's mother died of cancer a few years ago, and that was probably one of the first times that I was grateful we had built the business for more than money. Lana's parents had been married for thirty-seven years. It happened suddenly. We were going out to Alberta almost monthly for business, so we got to visit a lot.

We found out in late November that she had cancer and that she was going to pass away, and she was gone in early January. Thankfully, Lana was out there every week during that time. She would fly there on Monday and fly back on Friday.

The sad thing was, Lana's dad couldn't just stop working. When he found out his wife had cancer, he couldn't just say, "Okay, I'm done." He had to wait until the final two weeks to get off work and spend time with his wife. It broke my heart because here was this guy—so successful, thirty-seven years of marriage—and he was timing it over a couple grand a month.

After she passed away, everyone gathered around for a week. But then, inevitably, everyone eventually went home. After all the friends and family were gone, there was a Monday when he got up and went to work.

It gets dark in Edmonton around 4:00 p.m. at that time of year, and he would have come home to a dark house, with no one to greet him, and made his own meal. He would have sat at the table by himself, and I think that's when it really would have hit him. I can't imagine how lonely that would have been.

But that's not what happened. Lana was able to go out there and make him dinner and be there with him. I think that her being there helped him get through that tough time.

This may seem like a little thing, but it isn't. These are the kinds of opportunities that open up to us when we succeed in business. It's about much more than money. We can spend more time with the people we love most and deepen those relationships. And I think that's a cause worth fighting for.

Be Resilient

Another mistake people make, besides wanting things to be easy, is to choose low resiliency. Here's what I want you to understand: As you strive to become successful in your life's purpose, you're going to have plenty of reasons to quit.

I remember a couple in our business who got into a bit of a tax situation. The tax collectors said, "You owe us this much money." The couple insisted they didn't. The accountants looked and agreed that they didn't owe the money and told the couple that the auditor wasn't aware of one specific detail and that it would come out—and they wouldn't owe anything.

But it took two months to get it all resolved, and every single night these people got more negative, and they built the problem up as reason to give up. They started getting cranky with everyone they worked with, and finally they just quit.

About two weeks later the problem got fixed. But they had burned themselves, and their relationships, and lost the opportunity.

I was sad for them, and I said, "Man, they've had some colds longer than they stuck with that problem." We will all have reasons to put away our hacky sack and go home. We will all have reasons to be negative.

But to succeed in anything, we need to be resilient. We need to be tough. We need to go out there and understand that we're not just doing something important for money. We're doing it to make a difference. If the only time you get work done is when you feel okay, you're not going to make it in anything. We need to show up every day and do our best—or we're never going to succeed.

So often people tell me they'll try building a business for six months. I don't know why they nearly always say six months, instead of a year or eighteen months, but they do. Anyway, when someone tells me they'll make an effort for six months, I respond, "Don't try that with pregnancy."

Some things take more than six months. People who try things for a short time aren't really committed. The ones who succeed in life are those who keep going regardless of what obstacles come. How many NHL players or Olympic athletes said they'd give their sport a try for six months?

I think too often we look at successful business owners and attribute their success to intelligence, talent, connections, luck, their parents, or whatever. That may be true for a tiny percentage of people (and I don't know that I'd call them successful anyway, unless they do a lot with what they inherited). But we think these things when we see successful people at the end of their journey.

What we don't see is what it took to get them there. The real key to success is to do the right things and just keep on doing them.

Stick to It!

Success is more about tenacity than talent, more about perseverance than intelligence. Those who stick with it until they succeed may appear smarter—but it's because they've learned more than those who were unwilling to do the hard things. As Thomas Edison said, "Genius is 1 percent inspiration and 99 percent perspiration."

Consider the case of Marie Curie. She and her husband, French physicist Pierre, worked *in an old, abandoned, leaky shed without funds and without outside encouragement or help,* trying to isolate radium from a low-grade uranium ore called pitchblende.

After their 487th experiment had failed, Pierre threw up his hands in despair and said, "It will never be done. Maybe in a hundred years, but never in my day."

Marie confronted him and said, "If it takes a hundred years, it will be a pity, but I will not cease to work for it as long as I live." She was, of course, eventually successful, and countless cancer patients have benefited greatly from her perseverance.

Consider these other examples of famous "failures":

- Thomas Edison's teachers said he was "too stupid to learn anything." He was fired from his first two jobs for being "nonproductive." As an inventor, Edison made 1,000 unsuccessful attempts at inventing the light bulb. When a reporter asked, "How did it feel to fail 1,000 times?" Edison replied, "I didn't fail 1,000 times. The light bulb was an invention with 1,000 steps."
- Louis Pasteur was only a mediocre pupil in undergraduate studies and ranked fifteenth out of twenty-two students in chemistry.
- Henry Ford failed and went broke five times before he succeeded.
- R. H. Macy failed seven times before his store in New York City caught on.

- F. W. Woolworth was not allowed to wait on customers when he worked in a dry goods store because, his boss said, "He didn't have enough sense."

- When Bell telephone was struggling to get started, its owners offered all their rights to Western Union for $100,000. The offer was disdainfully rejected with the comment, "What use could this company make of an electrical toy?"

- Michael Jordan and Bob Cousy were each cut from their high school basketball teams. Jordan once observed, "I've failed over and over again in my life. That is why I succeed."

- Leo Tolstoy flunked out of college. He was described as both "unable and unwilling to learn."

- Twenty-seven publishers rejected Dr. Seuss's first book, *To Think That I Saw It on Mulberry Street*.

- Jack London received six hundred rejection slips before he sold his first story.

- *Chicken Soup for the Soul*, by Jack Canfield and Mark Victor Hansen, was rejected by over 140 publishers before one believed in it. That first book in the *Chicken Soup* series eventually sold eight million copies in forty-one languages. Years later, Jack Canfield said in an interview about the process, "I believe sometimes life sends us huge challenges to help us develop personal qualities such as courage, patience, perseverance, optimism and faith....Some people said it was not my destiny or karma to have that book published....What if I had given up after 100 rejections because it was my karma or it was my destiny? No, I believe we have a lot of power over our future and it is up to us to exercise that power."

It's Never Too Late to Start Again

If you've ever quit or done anything to disappoint yourself, understand that "it's never too late to be who you might have been," as George Eliot said. You're not licked until you stop trying. "Our greatest glory," said Confucius, "is not in never falling but in rising every time we fall." H. G. Wells added, "If you fell down yesterday, stand up today."

Lana says that restarts are her best friend because if she can just start again tomorrow, it makes everything okay. In the classic Canadian youth book *Anne of Green Gables*, the title character explains that she loves tomorrow because "it's always new, with no mistakes in it"—no mistakes in it yet.

Anne is a little orphan girl who has had everything against her since she was a baby, and even when luck starts to shine on her, she has an unparalleled knack for getting into "scrapes." But she knows that she can reset her success ticker by choosing to *keep* trying tomorrow and every other tomorrow.

Eventually she reaches her success, accomplishes her dreams, and even gets better at not getting into scrapes, but she does this by knowing what she stands for and never giving up for any reason, even when there are all kinds of excuses right in front of her.

The person you could become is always waiting for you, and it's worth finding out who that person is. People tend to focus so much more on what they want to *do* instead of who they want to *be*. It's important to not only build our business or career but to also build ourselves.

As Lana puts it, "I would rather fail a thousand times to see what I'm truly capable of than live my life wondering what could be."

> **"I would rather fail a thousand times to see what I'm truly capable of than live my life wondering what could be."**
> **—Lana Hamilton**

Failure is a temporary condition. There's no shame in trying and failing. The only shame is when you stop trying. As James Michener said, "Character consists of what you do on the third and fourth tries." I love that quote. It gets to the heart of what toughness is all about.

Get Tougher by Thinking Longer

Our tenacity and resiliency increase with our time and perspective. If we can visualize our future success, we can make better choices today about how we spend our time, effort, and money. And those small sacrifices today result in major long-term benefits down the road.

The easiest thing I've ever done in my life is build wealth. It is the easiest thing. All we did was start thinking long-term and applying the principles of success for a little bit, and some rewards started trickling in. These small results excited me, and I believed even more. Each time we improved our long-term approach, we experienced positive results in our business.

> **If we can visualize our future success, we can make better choices today about how we spend our time, effort, and money.**

Being broke is the hardest, most stressful thing I've ever done in my life. If you have the choice to live paycheck to paycheck or drink and smoke heavily, it may just be better for your health if you drink and smoke. I'm not promoting that; I'm just saying living paycheck to paycheck is one of the hardest ways there is to live.

Actually, for a lot of people, living paycheck to paycheck and drinking too much seem to go together. But you can choose not to live like that.

I remember working with a couple who didn't open their mail for six months because they didn't want to see their bills. They actually got to the point where their power was turned off before they finally opened their mail. Lo and behold, when they finally did open their mail, they found a $700 tax rebate. That could have saved their power bill! But they didn't find it until four months after it came.

Delayed gratification is not when you don't buy something because you can't afford it. It's when you *can* afford to buy something, but you *don't*.

If you can become an expert at delayed gratification, you can have whatever you want. Imagine if we could get our friends and relatives to admire us for our financial discipline! Instead, too many of us try to get them to admire us for the stuff we have on credit.

The farthest most people think ahead is two weeks; they're trained to think like that because that's how often they get paid. But as soon as you help people think ahead a little bit farther than they're used to, they can start changing their lives.

And it's about more than just being able to schedule things in advance. It's about being able to *prioritize* how we spend our time. I remember calling up one guy to invite him to an event six weeks away. I gave him the pitch and told him how great it was going to be. He said, "I'm sorry, but I've got a prior commitment that day."

I thought, "Seriously? Six weeks from now? Did you make another commitment more important than your wife and kids, your family and your country? What are you doing that's more important than building your future and helping people?"

So I said, "Yeah? What are you doing that day?"

He said "Oh, well, I'm volunteering for the SPCA [Society for the Prevention of Cruelty to Animals] that day."

Now, I'm all for dogs and cats and stuff, but I said, "Could you do it another day? Can you trade your shift or something?" But he doesn't think like that. He just does what's there on any given day.

He doesn't prioritize; he just takes his commitments on a first-come, first-served basis, which means he ends up serving everybody else's priorities and not getting anywhere with his own goals in life. His life gets harder over the long term because he doesn't want to make some hard decisions today.

We have to look ahead and see the long-term consequences of our choices today. When we do, we discover wells of tenacity inside us. We make better decisions in the present when we're working for a brighter future.

Unless we know what we want and engage the tenacity to go get it, life is one big disappointing merry-go-round. We're trapped in a circus over which we feel like we have no control. I say get your drunk self off the merry-go-round! Know what you want and have the guts to go after it! Let's toughen up.

*The grueling price to pay for living a life of greatness is
nothing compared to the awful cost of living small.*
—Stephen Palmer

CONCLUSION

"If you take the easy way out, life gets harder.
But if you take the hard way out, life gets easier."

I told you my story about hitchhiking to Edmonton. I told you
how that was the turning point in my business, the point of true
commitment. But I didn't tell you the full story.

What I haven't told you yet is that before I left, I FedExed my
suit to Lana's parents' house in Edmonton, so that I'd have a fresh,
clean suit to wear to the event when I got there. It kind of freaked
them out, getting an unexpected package from me with nothing
but my suit in it.

So I showed up at their house to pick up my suit before the
evening meeting. I didn't have money for a hotel room; in fact, I
hadn't even thought it through that much. I was just so consumed
with getting there, and I had the faith that something would work
out. The truth is I was kind of hoping my in-laws would take me
in.

It didn't quite work out that way. My mother-in-law kicked
me out. She was furious. She said, "How dare you do this to Lana?
What is your life like that you have to walk to Edmonton? You are
ruining my daughter's life. And you are not welcome in my home."

I had to walk from their house back to the hotel where the event was. I had to ask someone if I could bunk up with them in their hotel room, which was humiliating.

Lana told me that she called her mom, and she had to sit down because she was shaking so bad, scared to death of talking to her. She said, "Mom, what did you do that for? What did you do that for? He just walked to Edmonton."

And she said, "Lana, your family has to take care of you. And if this is what he is doing to you, then he is not welcome in your family."

Lana responded, "Mom, he *is* my family, and he is fighting hard to give our family a future. And if he is not welcome in your home, then I am not welcome in your home either."

That experience was so hard. But I know it's nothing compared to how hard my life would be today had I not made that choice then.

I believed what W. L. Bateman said: "If you keep on doing what you've always done, you'll keep on getting what you've always got." Well, I was bone tired of getting what I'd been getting. I wanted something different, so I knew I had to *do* something different.

> **I was bone tired of getting what I'd been getting. I wanted something different, so I knew I had to *do* something different.**

One time when I was mentoring a couple, the phone rang. The man answered it, and it was a bill collector, so he handed the phone over to his wife. That six-dollar-an-hour punk on the other line berated, thrashed, and stressed her for the next ten minutes.

I was shocked that the husband just sat there talking to me like nothing was going on. By the time she got off the phone, she was almost in tears. I mean, if someone had treated her like that on the street, the husband probably would have punched him out.

I asked him, "Why didn't *you* take that call? If you're going to succeed, you shouldn't let some strange guy verbally beat up on your wife. You've got to toughen up and deal with things like this yourself."

Sometimes we get so comfortable with our situation that we don't realize we need to toughen up. I hope *you* are so *uncomfortable* with your current situation that you're willing to fight for something different and better. I hope you're hungry enough to toughen up—because the world desperately needs you to. The world desperately needs you to become the person you could be.

It's going to be hard. There will be times when you'll look silly—like the time I drove with some associates to speak at an event in Boston. After a long, hard weekend, we went to a gas station to fuel up. I told the guys, "I'll drive as far as I can. I can probably get us to the border." I stocked up on coffee and energy drinks, and I drank so much in the store that before I even paid for the stuff, I had to go to the bathroom again.

By the time we got to the tolls to leave the city, my friends were already asleep in the back. I pulled up to the toll booth. I must have put the coin in and then dropped off to sleep. My foot wasn't on the brake, so the car just kind of rolled off to the shoulder and luckily stopped. We all slept like logs for like seven hours. When I woke up, it was daylight, and the morning traffic was just starting to come through.

The other guys started to rouse, so I got back on the road. "Hey, where are we?" one of them asked.

I shrugged. "I dunno."

> I can't promise you that you won't ever look like an idiot, that you won't ever lose sleep, that your family will always approve of what you're doing, or that your friends won't think you're nuts. But I can promise you this: if you stick with it, it will be worth more than you can imagine right now.

As Chris Brady says, "You gotta look like an idiot before you look cool." That was just one of many times when I looked like an idiot on my drive to success.

I can't promise you that you won't ever look like an idiot, that you won't ever lose sleep, that your family will always approve of what you're doing, or that your friends won't think you're nuts. But I can promise you this: if you stick with it, it will be worth more than you can imagine right now.

So when it gets hard and you're not sure you can make it, pull yourself up by your bootstraps and remember the Eight Strengths:

1. Attitude
2. Courage
3. Character
4. Duty
5. Honor
6. Relationships
7. Passion
8. Tenacity

Declare an intention. Then stick with that intention while you take your punishment. And keep going—no matter what. As you do this, you'll have a life that is great and fun. That's right: *fun*! If you do the hard things now, your life will become much, much easier in the long run.

I think real toughness is well described in Rudyard Kipling's great poem "If":

If you can keep your head when all about you
Are losing theirs and blaming it on you;
If you can trust yourself when all men doubt you,
But make allowance for their doubting too;

If you can wait and not be tired by waiting,
Or being lied about, don't deal in lies,
Or being hated, don't give way to hating,
And yet don't look too good, nor talk too wise;

If you can dream—and not make dreams your master;
If you can think—and not make thoughts your aim;
If you can meet with Triumph and Disaster
And treat those two imposters just the same;

If you can bear to hear the truth you've spoken
Twisted by knaves to make a trap for fools,
Or watch the things you gave your life to, broken,
And stoop and build 'em up with worn-out tools;

If you can make one heap of all your winnings
And risk it on one turn of pitch-and-toss,
And lose, and start again at your beginnings
And never breathe a word about your loss;

If you can force your heart and nerve and sinew
To serve your turn long after they are gone,
And so hold on when there is nothing in you
Except the Will which says to them: "Hold on!"

If you can talk with crowds and keep your virtue,
Or walk with Kings—nor lose the common touch;
If neither foes nor loving friends can hurt you;
If all men count with you, but none too much;

If you can fill the unforgiving minute
With sixty seconds' worth of distance run,
Yours is the Earth and everything that's in it,
And—which is more—you'll be a Man, my son!

Please don't do what many readers do and skip the poem. The words in this poem matter. Like shining shoes, reading the little things is the way we prepare for greatness. So if you didn't read this poem closely, go back and do it.

Think about each line, and apply it to your life.

The thing is each of us has a truly great person inside, a really great man or woman, a genuinely great leader. We just need to be our best.

> **A great life is in each of us, if only we'll toughen up and go after it. We can't let anything stand in the way.**

Too often, the main thing holding us back is that we lack toughness in some way. But we can overcome this roadblock. We have to, or we won't live up to our potential. A great life is in each of us, if only we'll toughen up and go after it. We can't let anything stand in the way.

As the poem says, real toughness will give you the world and everything in it; toughness can lead you to all the financial freedom, business success, and family happiness you could ever want. But even more importantly, it will give you *yourself.* By choosing to live this path—the tough path, the *right* path—you are choosing to be your real and best self. You are consciously taking responsibility for making you who you should be.

The truth is we are stronger than we know. We can be better

> **The truth is we are stronger than we know.**

than we may have imagined. And the world needs us. It needs us in so many ways. It needs us to stand up and be our best. It needs more and better leaders—and it needs each of us to give our all.

We've gotten used to wimping out far too often, but that's not who we really are. We are meant to lead. We are meant to do and build great things. And now is the time. Now is the time to stop making any excuses. Now is the time to clarify our vision and purpose and drastically improve the world. Now is the time to take great action.

All of this will only happen when we understand one thing: Now is the time to toughen up—because that call to greatness will come. In one way or another, someone in our lives will call out, "Man overboard!" And we'll have to decide what to do.

Some people will sit there and hope others take action.

But not you. You'll jump up and sprint to the call for help. You'll reach deep down inside and find your greatness. You'll do the little things each day that prepare you for great choices when the going gets tough. You'll work hard, you'll refuse to give up, and you'll help many others succeed right along with you.

All of this will happen because you'll refuse to give up or give in. You'll take whatever challenges come, and you'll just keep on doing the right thing. That's toughness, and that's what you're about. That's who you are.

That's who we all are, when we get right down to it. It's time for each of us, and our whole generation, to stand up and toughen up.

Fight fiercely.

Yours in victory…

Claude Hamilton

Acknowledgments

The collaboration of many creative minds and passionate souls goes into producing a book, and I want to offer my sincere appreciation to all those who have contributed to this one.

I am especially grateful for Oliver DeMille's significant contribution to the construct and content of this work. Thanks are also due to Orrin and Laurie Woodward, Chris and Terri Brady, Tim and Amy Marks, Bill and Jackie Lewis, Dan and Lisa Hawkins, George and Jill Guzzardo, Wayne and Raylene MacNamara, Curtis and Debbie Spolar, Holger and Lindsey Spiewak, Joce and Cynthia Dionne, Terry and Ann Franks, Alex and Leighann Nickerson, Denis and Lisa Leger, Scott Staley, Stuart and Carrianne Hall, and Jean and Tamie Belanger.

Deborah Brady, Wendy Branson, and the rest of the editors at Obstaclés Press did a tremendous job on editing the book. I am very thankful to Norm Williams for an excellent job on the layout and design and Sonya Beeler for the fantastic cover artwork and cartoons. Bill Rousseau helped to keep the whole project on track. And as usual, Rob Hallstrand did an exceptional job coordinating all of the various efforts at Obstaclés Press.

Most of all, I want to thank my wife Lana for being the toughest woman I know and the best partner I could have in business and in life. You and our sons Wyatt and Gryffin motivate me daily to stay tough and keep striving to be the best husband, father, and leader I can be. And, of course, I am forever grateful to my Lord and Savior Jesus Christ for His great sacrifice and being the best model of toughness and love any of us could ever have.

I honor all of you for your inspiration and assistance in bringing this project to fruition and helping me tell my story in a way that can touch lives and make a difference in this world.

Notes

1 Winston Churchill, in an address to the students at Harrow School in October 1941.

2 Robert Frost, "The Road Less Travelled."

3 William Shakespeare, *Julius Caesar,* Act 2, Scene 2.

4 Marcus Aurelius, *Meditations.*

5 James Allen, *As a Man Thinketh.*

6 Viktor Frankl, *Man's Search for Meaning.*

7 See *Treasury of Spiritual Wisdom: A Collection of 10,000 Inspirational Quotes,* compiled by Andy Zubko.

8 Thomas Paine, *The Crisis.*

9 Kenneth Blanchard, Donald Carew, and Eunice Parisi-Carew, *The One-Minute Manager Builds High Performance Teams,* 21.

10 Henry David Thoreau, *Walden.*

11 Quoted in A. R. Orage, "Talks with Katherine Mansfield at Fontainebleau," *The Century Magazine,* November 1924.

12 Roy B. Zuck, *The Speaker's Quote Book.*

13 William Shakespeare, *Henry V,* Act 4, Scene 3.

14 Quote attributed to J. R. R. Tolkein.

15 Nelson Mandela, *Long Walk to Freedom.*

16 André Gide, *Oscar Wilde: Reminiscences.*

17 Plato's *Republic.*

18 Frederic Bastiat, *The Law.*

19 Definitions are from the *Compact Oxford English Dictionary.*

20 A. A. Milne, *Lunch.*

21 Fyodor Dostoyevsky, *The Adolescent.*

22 Ronald Reagan, quoted in *Observer,* March 29, 1981.

23 Martin Luther King Jr., "I Have a Dream," 1963.

24 CoachWooden.com.

25 Quoted in *Lincoln's Imagination,* by Noah Brooks, *Scribner's Monthly,* August 1879.

26 *Quotes by Thomas Paine,* Quotationsbook.com.

27 *Helen Keller's Journal: 1936–1937*

28 Yann-Brice Dherbier and Pierre-Henri Verlhac, eds., *Paul Newman: A Life in Pictures.*

29 Friedrich Nietzsche, *Twilight of the Idols.*

30 Henry James, *The Portrait of a Lady.*

31 As quoted in Gary Ninneman, *C.I.A.: Church in Atrophy.*

32 Terry Goodkind, *Confessor.*

33 Joan Didion, *On Self Respect.*

34 Harper Lee, *To Kill a Mockingbird.*

35 Marcus Aurelius, *Meditations,* Book X.

36 Frederick Douglass, *Narrative of the Life of Frederick Douglass, an American Slave.*

37 Mortimer Adler, *The Great Books of the Western World,* volume 1, 358.

38 Ibid., 359.

39 Luke 22:42.

40 George Eliot, *Middlemarch.*

41 Mortimer Adler, *The Great Books of the Western World,* volume 1, 361.

42 John F. Kennedy, *Profiles in Courage.*

43 George MacDonald, *The Wise Woman and Other Stories.*

44 Mark Batterson, *Soulprint: Discovering Your Divine Destiny.*

45 Letter to the Bishops, Clergy, and Laity of the Protestant Episcopal Church in the States of New York, New Jersey, Pennsylvania, Delaware, Maryland, Virginia, and North Carolina, August 1789.

46 Terry Jones, "Kariya's a knockout," *The Calgary Herald,* June 8, 2003.

47 Ibid.

48 Abraham Lincoln, Cooper Union Address, February 27, 1860, New York, New York, copyright 2013 Abraham Lincoln Online, http://www.abrahamlincolnonline.org/lincoln/speeches/cooper.htm.

49 George S. Patton Jr., *Federal Troops in Domestic Disturbances.*

50 Ben Stein's Column, August 9, 2004.

51 Dr. Suess, *Horton Hatches the Egg.*

52 Online Etymology Dictionary.

53 *Great Books of the Western World,* v. 1, 729.

54 Ibid., 728.

55 Ibid., 744.

56 *Compact Oxford English Dictionary*, 309.

57 Ibid., 485.

58 Ibid., 309, under "dutiful."

59 Stephen Covey, *The 7 Habits of Highly Effective People.*

60 James Bowman, *Honor: A History,* 1–3.

61 Donald Miller, *A Million Miles in a Thousand Years: What I Learned While Editing My Life.*

62 Nicholas Sparks, *Safe Haven.*

63 Nicholas Sparks, *At First Sight.*

64 Nicholas Sparks, *Dear John.*

65 As quoted in *From Telegraph to Light Bulb with Thomas Edison* (2007) by Deborah Hedstrom.

66 The Official Website of Amelia Earhart, www.ameliaearhart.com.